Just Chevys

TRUE TALES & ICONIC CARS FROM AMERICA'S NO. 1 AUTO MAKER

Copyright ©2010 F+W Media, Inc.

All rights reserved. No portion of this publication may be reproduced or transmitted in any form or by any means, electronic or mechanical, including photocopy, recording, or any information storage and retrieval system, without permission in writing from the publisher, except by a reviewer who may quote brief passages in a critical article or review to be printed in a magazine or newspaper, or electronically transmitted on radio, television, or the Internet.

Published by

kp fwmedia

Krause Publications, a division of F+W Media, Inc.
700 East State Street • Iola, WI 54990-0001
715-445-2214 • 888-457-2873
www.krausebooks.com

To order books or other products call toll-free 1-800-258-0929
or visit us online at www.krausebooks.com or www.Shop.Collect.com

Library of Congress Control Number: 2010925534

ISBN-13: 978-1-4402-1425-7
ISBN-10: 1-4402-1425-5

Designed by Sharon Bartsch
Edited by Brian Earnest

Printed in the United States of America

CONTENTS

FOREWORD 4
CHAPTER 1 1917 Chevy 5
CHAPTER 2 1920 Four-Ninety 8
CHAPTER 3 1935 Chevrolet Oil Test 12
CHAPTER 4 1936 Chevrolets 16
CHAPTER 5 1938 Chevy Coupe Barn Find 22
CHAPTER 6 1941 Cabriolet 26
CHAPTER 7 1941 Options 28
CHAPTER 8 1949 Chevy Kick-Off 33
CHAPTER 9 1953 Bel Air Wagon 36
CHAPTER 10 1953 Stepvan 41
CHAPTER 11 1955 Biscayne Show Car 47
CHAPTER 12 1955 Bel Air Sedan 52
CHAPTER 13 1957 Bel Air Sedan 56
CHAPTER 14 1958 Chevrolet Lineup 64
CHAPTER 15 1959 Impala Convertible 69
CHAPTER 16 1960 Chevy Impala 73
CHAPTER 17 1960 Corvair 76
CHAPTER 18 1961 Corvair Greenbrier 81
CHAPTER 19 1962 Chevy II 85
CHAPTER 20 1962 Impala Coupe 88
CHAPTER 21 1965-69 Corvair 90
CHAPTER 22 1966 Chevelle 94
CHAPTER 23 1966 Corvette Sting Ray 98
CHAPTER 24 1968 Chevelle SS Restoration 103
CHAPTER 25 1968 Chevelle SS 106
CHAPTER 26 1969 Fred Gibb Camaro 112
CHAPTER 27 1969 Camaro Z/28 117
CHAPTER 28 1969 Corvette 123
CHAPTER 29 1970 Corvette 127
CHAPTER 30 1970s Nova 130
CHAPTER 31 1971 Rally Nova 133
CHAPTER 32 1975 Chevys 136

FOREWORD
By Angelo Van Bogart

Chevrolet: The people pleaser

In 2007, General Motors launched an ad campaign that spoke a great truth — people who love cars love Chevy. It's an affection that is deserved, for few other automakers can claim the dependability, flexibility and accessibility that makes Chevrolets fun to own and fun to drive.

Chevrolet cars and trucks have always offered a high level of quality at a relatively low price. Their engines are often easily built and economically maintained, and even handily modified. A strong dealer network and aftermarket parts sources makes Chevrolets and their parts easy to find, and within reach. Add it all up and it's easy to see why Chevrolet is so wildly popular.

Much of Chevrolet's strength has also come from its diversity. The bow-tie emblem dresses family sedans, heavy- and light-duty trucks, sports and race cars and everything in between, all touting the dependability and economy of operation hard-working people need from their vehicles. And Chevrolet has been doing it since 1927.

Chevrolet was founded in the very root of diversity. The company was started by William Crapo Durant in 1911 after he was ousted from the helm of General Motors, the same corporation he founded. Durant selected race car driver Louis Chevrolet to design a car and for whom Crapo had it named. In just two years, the duo split; Louis Chevrolet wanted his name to grace an expensive high-performance car. Durant sought an inexpensive Model T fighter that would produce the sales needed for him to retake General Motors. Ironically, both would eventually have their Chevrolet, but it would take until the 1950s.

By the Ike era, the economical and dependable Chevrolet saw the addition of the Corvette sports car. The Chevrolet could be had as a utilitarian One-Fifty or Biscayne or a gilded Bel Air or Impala. Engine options varied from a fuel-sipping straight-six to a petrol-chugging dual-quad small block or tri-power big block. Exotic fuel-injection engines bridged the 1950s and 1960s, when Chevrolet's automotive line began expanding from a single menu of full-size cars and the specialty Corvette to also include compact Corvairs and Novas, mid-size Chevelles and muscular Camaros.

Today, there remains a Chevrolet for everyone. Luxury is available from a full-size Impala. Utility can be found in a Silverado or Suburban. Economy is available with an Aveo or the upcoming Volt. A sporty spirit is just a turn of the key away in a Camaro or Corvette. All offer a rare combination of economy and dependability found in few other vehicles.

Some of the hobby's most beloved Chevrolets have been included in this book, their stories torn from the pages of *Old Cars Weekly*. Hopefully, their stories are as fun to read as owning and driving a Chevrolet.

CHAPTER 1 — 1917 CHEVY

Story by Gerald Perschbacher

1917'S 'HOT ONE'
Chevrolet toyed with V-8 power long before the '50s

This delightful Chevrolet "D" touring car carries the famous early V-8 engine. Chevrolet expert mechanic Rick Quirin of Belleville, Ill., admires the V-8 for its overall construction and performance.

When you're hot, you're hot! So it was with Chevrolet in 1917.

"The Four-Ninety model as it is being built today, offers without exception the greatest car value of the 1917 season," said the Chevrolet sales manager for the Kansas City region. But there was more about which he bragged.

"Sample 'F' models will be delivered, we believe, this month; sample 'D' models next month, or early in January."

"Sample" was his term for "demonstrator," but there's more to the story behind the models he delineated.

The Four-Ninety was the aggressive model for Chevrolet. It became the quantity leader for the brand, lowest priced in the entire lineup. The Four-Ninety was for the first-time car owner who had trouble spending mega bucks on fancy cars or who didn't

5

know a clutch from a throttle. Its cone clutch allowed for relatively easy shifting, as long as the leather portion was properly oiled and in good condition. The H-pattern shift was to become standard for nearly all American cars in future years. The Four-Ninety wasn't as easy to drive as expensive cars five or more times its price, but it was a heck of a lot easier than working the controls and pedals of a Model T Ford.

The Four-Ninety rode on a wheelbase of 102 inches for 1917. That gave it spunk and maneuverability in tight spaces, especially for citified parking. The "F" series for 1917 came as the F2 (Royal Mail roadster) running a 108-inch wheelbase, and the F5 (Baby Grand touring) on the same stretch.

Chevrolet's foray beyond fours

Until then, the Chevrolet line consisted of four-cylinder engines, but the top brains at the company wanted more. Chevrolet was settling in as top dog among General Motors brands, having joined the bunch in 1915. Call it a test, an experiment, a risk or a dream, but Chevrolet rolled out its "D" series for 1917. And it was a honey. Riding regally on a 120-inch wheelbase, the "D" came as chummy roadster and as touring car. But greatest of all, it carried a V-8 engine.

Twice as good as the lesser Chevrolets, you might reason. Well, why not? Cadillac had relinquished any desire for a four-cylinder car when it launched its new V-8 in 1914. The implication: the V-8 was double any four. Luxury marques, such as Packard, had jumped ahead of the pack in 1915 with the Twin Six, twice the performance of the luxury sixes that had dominated the market. Cadillac also hinted its extra two cylinders made any six as antiquated as a pair of spats at a hip-hop party.

Maybe the time for a V-8 wasn't right for Chevrolet. Perhaps its engineering needed more tweaking. Its engine could have provided a mixed message that confused luxury with low-priced motoring. Might have been too much internal competition within GM. For these potential reasons and others unmentioned, the first-generation Chevrolet V-8 Model "D" quietly faded into history after the 1919 versions. Chevrolet would go back to the V-8 with the 1955 model year.

The Kansas City general manager was aiming to make 1917 a banner year. In polite form he wrote, "If there is anything that writing can do which our dealers believe will aid them in any way at any time, do not hesitate to apprise him fully. We are strengthening our sales organization in every way and our service department is likewise being extended. We want satisfied Chevrolet owners everywhere, and it is the intention of this branch to see that they are satisfied."

Chevrolet's key to success

An early element of success that was discovered too late by too many carmakers was so simple it was overlooked. It involved servicing the car. When buggies, wagons and carriages plied the roads, their service was usually handled by blacksmiths or some other local expert capable of the task. Wagon and carriage makers usually stayed out of such business and simply provided vehicles.

When cars came along, the task of servicing took remarkably different tact. The basics of wheels and axles could be easily handled by locals, but engines were a different matter. So were pneumatic tires, transmissions, clutches and magnetos. Now maintenance required knowledge, manuals, hands-on training. It also required accessibility to replacement parts. These factors put the automobile in a far different camp than buggies and carriages.

Car owners needed a support system. Some makers, weary just with the making of cars, seemed to think that someone "out there" would magically be imbued with the abilities to instigate a proper, long-lasting and safe repair. Those companies faded away quickly as owner loyalty drained with the first or second major repair.

Some companies offered little information on how to rebuild or install replacement parts. They felt as though some magic wand would wave above the head of a car owner once the purchase had been made. It wasn't their responsibility as a carmaker, was it?

Companies that took this line of thought merely helped the rise of repair literature, such as the Dyke manuals of yore. Offered to the general public, these instructive tomes — often thick with well-illustrated pages of technical information, theories, schematics and tips — filled the gap by offering correspondence courses on every pertinent subject of motor maintenance, diagnostics and operational safety.

Successful makers took a radical route to train field personnel, via authorized dealers. It was the safer plan to follow — safer for car owners and safer for the manufacturer. It also encouraged ongoing contact with the owner, who might be a potential repeat customer when the time came to buy another car. However, in long-ranging applications, this last idea was still in the development stage in 1917. There were still numerous families that had yet to buy their first automobile.

Said the Kansas City manager, "We are having service representatives in every state we control to instruct our dealers to take care of mechanical troubles as they find them, and in every way do what is necessary to build up the strongest and best liked sales and service policies of any automobile company in the country, barring none."

Chevrolet was the "hot one" for 1917. Positioning for the future, the marque was moving from success to success.

Some of the brand's best years were yet to come, and those would be some of its hottest ever!

CHAPTER 2 | **1920 FOUR-NINETY**

By Gerald Perschbacher

A LITTLE CHEVROLET BEAT PIKE'S PEAK IN 1920

Chevrolet proved the prowess of all of its 1920 models when William Bentrup took a stripped Chevrolet Four-Ninety up Pike's Peak in record time for its class.

In the early 1800s, Pike's Peak challenged explorers. Towering over the rugged southwest landscape, Zebulon Pike himself said the summit would never be conquered by man. Little did he realize that automobiles would reach the height about a century later.

By 1920, automakers saw Pike's Peak as a challenge of endurance, performance and speed. The manufacturer that set a new record reaching the top would certainly revel in the light of positive publicity. This would equate to good sales as people flocked to dealerships to see the model that tamed a new speed record.

Thus, Chevrolet set out to conquer Pike's Peak on Labor Day of 1920. By that year, thousands made the upward trek to the summit by car, enjoyed the spectacular view, and descended.

A Chevrolet official noted that the invention of the automobile was one of the greatest boons to mankind. The people reaching the top of the peak "traveled in automobiles, the invention that is no respecter of obstacles and that has made its own roads over mountain, plain and valley in a manner that our forefathers never dreamed possible."

What assisted in the climb was the Pike's Peak Automobile Highway, completed in 1915. Graded and wide enough for safe travel, it still posed a challenge for cars to set new ascent records. The road made a special competition event possible: the Penrose Cup Hill Climb, which made the road world famous. The road was not easy to traverse. It had numerous curves and "W's." The grade averaged 10 degrees and at times went as steep as 17.

"The Weaver-Porter Co., Chevrolet dealers in Colorado Springs, Colo., had been getting such excellent reports from Chevrolet cars that had climbed the peak during the tourist season that they discussed the race with their chief mechanic, William Bentrup. He knew the road," reported Chevrolet's home office. "He also knew Chevrolet cars. He jumped at the opportunity to enter the event."

In times of good weather, there was little danger to life, and just as little danger for the company. If a car made good on the summit, glory was assured. Those that failed simply vanished into history. Given the factor for low risk, the chances were good for a Chevrolet to make a strong showing. Just finishing the run spoke well of any make, and if a Chevrolet could score in the top four or five cars, it was all the better.

Bentrup selected a stock Four-Ninety touring car. The model had been introduced for 1916 and had proved its merits in the hands of thousands of owners since. Four-Ninety Chevrolets had pulled hills, conquered streams, worked in fields, delivered doctors to house calls, hauled modest loads, and gave wings to family vacations hither and yon. By 1920, it had become a mainstay amid the General Motors lineup. In fact, it seemed to be the corporation's future.

Bentrup's Four-Ninety touring car "had already run 7,000 miles in demonstration work" and was stripped for action, an official reported. Certain modifications were allowed. "Only the chassis was used. Wire wheels were installed. The gas tank was raised in front of the dash and the seat lowered lowered flush with the frame. No new bearings or parts were necessary, despite the punishment given a car in the trial tests up the steep and curved road."

The weather was far from good. In fact, at the foot of the mountain, the weather high up the peak appeared downright ominous. "Clouds hid the peak summit on that day of the race," said the official Chevrolet report. "It was only Sept. 6, but a blinding snow storm was raging, and a bitter wind blowing around the rocky cliffs 14,109 feet above sea level."

"The Chevrolet took each sharp curve with ease, and got away again at full speed. Slippery curves where other drivers before him had skidded were negotiated with apparent ease."

In spite of conditions, about 3,000 motor cars lined the highway, and an estimated crowd of 10,000 onlookers were on hand to view the contest called "the blue ribbon event of the West." Atop the mountain, hundreds of spectators were facing the blizzard just to have a prime seat to see the winner reach the terminus of the highway.

In 1920, there was "an imposing list of entries, with factory experts from eastern motor centers and professional pilots at the wheels," stated an on-scene reporter. "They practice for two weeks prior to the race. Bentrup made only two trial trips."

It was a time trial, which was still a speed race since the best speed meant the least time to the top. AAA monitored the race. Among contenders, the four-cylinder Chevrolet Four-Ninety drew the second to last position.

Every 10 minutes, a car would launch its bid for the top. Visually, each car was lost from sight due to pine trees along the road. At the end near the height of the peak, observers were communicating by telephone to officials at the starting line so everyone could know the results. It was a tense and exciting time.

Bentrup sped up the road once the starting sign was given. He drove alone. "No mechanic rode with him to pump oil and gasoline into a faltering motor," which gasped for oxygen amid the thin air environment. "No goggles shielded his eyes, and no elaborate trappings kept the wintry breezes from cutting to his marrow. He was out to win and wanted no surplus baggage," it was noted.

Call that danger. In bad weather, he risked life and limb and could have stalled along the route. Gravel surfaces could have given way in the inclement conditions. Any number of dangers might have plagued his assent. But the Chevrolet driver was determined.

"The Chevrolet took each sharp curve with ease, and got away again at full speed. Slippery curves where other drivers before him had skidded were negotiated with apparent ease. Fifteen to 17-degree grades leveled out before the stout little motor that never failed. The motometer showed a hot engine after 12 miles of upgrade, but she was not steaming.

"As he reached the summit with a straightaway of only 200 yards, Bentrup 'stepped on her' to the limit, the car leaped as if by command, and the race was over," noted Chevrolet. "Timers and judges of the finish of the annual Pike's Peak Hill Climb conferred, and the man with the megaphone shouted, "Bentrup in Chevrolet; time: 24 minutes, five and two-fifths seconds." The final car came in two minutes behind Bentrup.

He and the Four-Ninety took first in Class Number 1 for cars with a piston displacement of 183 inches or less.

The spectators gasped for more reason than one. Here was an upstart in the race, with no special support from the factory, competing against serious contenders with cars made ready for a victory. These were experienced drivers. Bentrup had bested them.

For his win, Bentrup claimed $500, but the victory meant much more to him, the dealership and the company. Leaders at General Motors broke into smiles. One of the least of their cars in high-speed performance had made its mark in major competition. For Bentrup, it was his first race and first victory which he would never forget.

Mr. Porter, one of the owners of the dealership that sponsored the Four-Ninety in the race, was ecstatic. It was reported that he had enough enthusiasm for the win as everyone else combined.

And what about officials at Chevrolet?

"The Chevrolet 'Four-Ninety' performance in the 1920 Pike's Peak Race was the best yet made by a car in its class," said the front office. Prospective buyers were told, "When you tour Colorado, make the trip up Pike's Peak, and see what it is to do it in 24 minutes — the Chevrolet 'Four-Ninety' time."

The stout little performer had boosted its reputation tremendously in one day. What's more, it re-emphasized the marque's early history, capturing the spirit of race car driver Louis Chevrolet — who was William Durant's inspiration as a corporate executive who had been cast down from the top official at General Motors. On the strength of Chevrolet, he reclaimed his post and envisioned major expansions that would place the corporation in the lead among peers.

As for the race and the peak, sometime in the late 1950s and early 1960s, Pike's Peak lost its luster as a site for car makers to boost their machines. The salt flats in Utah and elsewhere gained more note as outright high speeds became the record to beat, rather than agility in hugging a mountain road.

Yet, thanks to men like Bill Bentrup, a dealership with foresight, and the assembly line workers who constructed his Four-Ninety, an interesting little chapter in automotive history was written that Labor Day in 1920.

CHAPTER 3 | **1935 CHEVROLET OIL TEST**

Story and photo by Gerald Perschbacher

THE TEST OF MILES
Louis Chevrolet and Sun Oil proved new use of new oils with '35 Chevrolet

As Louis Chevrolet proved, a 1935 Chevrolet coach could run with 20W oil in the winter without negative results. He made his point in a 5,000-mile run.

It wasn't easy being Chevrolet in 1935. Its papa, General Motors, set high goals for the division. Like most children, Chevrolet would have to work its way there, using every bit of muscle to claim and hold top post as the nation's family-budget sales leader.

What did the brand offer? Two series: Standard (Series EC with 107-inch wheelbase) and Master Deluxe (Series ED/EA with 113-inch platform). Both ran the respected inline six with cast-iron block, three main bearings and overhead valves, as customers had come to expect when the engine bowed for 1929. Displacement was 206.8 cubic inches with braking horsepower of 74 at 3,200 rpm.

To please daddy, Chevrolet rolled out five Standard models (sport roadster, phaeton,

Knee-Action Ride on the 1935 Chevrolet was touted by a handful of specially made units with the mechanism lifted high for all to see in operation.

coupe, coach and sedan), while the Master Deluxe carried six (coupe, coach and sedan, plus sport coupe, sport sedan and town sedan). Standards ranged in price from $465 to $550, while Master Deluxes stepped up from $560 to $675. Not much difference in dollar spread by today's standards, but the difference was about 17-19 percent for the more well-endowed Master Deluxe.

In Master Deluxe guise, the 1935 Chevrolet offered Knee-Action Ride, a novel system for cushioning body jostle over rough roads. To promote the innovation, special demonstrator versions were made for public relations. The models had their front fenders cut back to allow extensions from the front suspension. Metal arms extended as high as the hood, with Knee-Action units atop. This allowed bystander, rider and driver the opportunity to watch how the mechanism worked.

Master Deluxe Chevrolets for 1935 also offered another improvement: Turret-top construction, advertised as steel protection for safety. Lesser offerings in the Chevrolet line had the composite top of old, still fine and usable, but not as marketable as all-steel tops. It was an era on the verge of all-steel bodies across the industry. But not yet.

Innovations. Good pricing. Wonderful dealer network. GM was proud of Chevy's success. But the parent also knew that any make of car is only as good as the current model. Reputations have been won or lost in a single sales year. So Chevrolet officials set out to put their favorite car front and center in the public eye.

It remains to be shown who it was that had the idea of taking a Chevrolet across country in late 1934 to prove the worth of light-weight engine oil. The car chosen by AAA to run the test was a Chevrolet two-door coach. The driver, of all people, was Louis Chevrolet, the famous race car driver who allowed his name and reputation to become a household fixture on GM's favorite low-priced car.

A stunt? Hardly. A practical exposé? Probably. Good for Chevrolet? Let the results speak.

First, the crankcase was sealed. No oil could be added. The point was to show the enduring properties of thinner oil, since "automobile dealers and garage men, in common with automobile owners, have long regarded thickness as one of the prime measures of an oil's lubricating quality, as well as its ability to 'stand up' under heavy service," said a reporter assigned to the drill. The test came on the heels of the introduction of winter-weight motor oil in 1933. Manufacturers were ready to push the idea of 10W and 20W oils as safe.

So it was that Sun Oil Co. sponsored the event in November of 1934 as the new '35 Chevrolets were heading toward showrooms. AAA supervised the test.

"The test was enough of a 'stunt' to arrest public attention, yet it was so rigidly supervised as to make its outcome thoroughly authenticated," it was noted. To make that happen, AAA observer H.H. Allen rode with Mr. Chevrolet. Sun Oil provided a photographer, but that was all. Of course, the Chevrolet motor car was the star at each stop, and the glamour of Mr. Chevrolet still rubbed off favorably onto the marque.

Average speed for the six-cylinder car was 42 mph. Preparation was made to assure no loss of oil from the engine due to gasket leakage or other means. Sunoco 20W oil was used. One little twist was added: special piston rings were installed (two No. 70, one No. 80 Perfect Circle brand). A new breather was installed, and the oil pan had a reinforced flange.

Louis Chevrolet left on Nov. 6. His trip took him through Norwood and Pittsburgh, Pa.; Canton, Ohio; Fort Wayne, Ind.; Detroit; Indianapolis; then to Miami through the Everglades, and back to Norwood. He registered 5,009.6 miles in 119 hours, 31 minutes. Gasoline consumption was 267.25 gallons (18.75 miles per gallon). No breakdowns or malfunctions marred the trip, which spoke well of the Chevrolet.

Of the 5.15 quarts of 20W engine oil in the motor, 1.46 quarts remained — "enough oil…for several hundred miles more, and the drained oil contained only fifteen-hundredths of one percent dirt and sludge. Oil consumption was 3.68 quarts, which is at the rate of 1,360 miles to the quart," it was reported.

After the run, AAA tore down the engine. According to Louis Chevrolet and AAA's Mr. Allen, the bearings, pistons and rings were still in "first-class condition." The wear was hardly measurable on the new car.

It was noted that "Mr. Chevrolet considers this test to be more exacting than speedway tests, because it involves maximum speeds considerably greater than the average speed." To maintain the average speed above 40 mph for the entire trip, Mr. Chevrolet drove long stretches at 50 mph. His conclusion: lightweight oil was fine for winter use and provided "perfect lubrication." He even concluded that 20W oil could be used in climates that were moderately warm, as was the case with his southern swing.

The race car legend further concluded that the 20W oil was fine for speeds below 50, but above that mark there were higher operating temperatures that stressed the oil's properties. A heavier oil for those severe conditions was suggested.

Said Mr. Chevrolet: "This test has proved to me that the recommendation of car manufacturers to use 20W oil for temperatures averaging as low as zero is the best contribution that has been made to the right kind of lubrication in winter, because undoubtedly, this oil will let motorists start much quicker and will give them 100 percent lubrication…something that motorists believed could not be done with such a light oil."

And a new Chevrolet was at the heart of the test, making its General Motors parent proud.

CHAPTER 4 | **1936 CHEVROLETS**

By Gerald Perschbacher

CHEVY SUCCESS
1936 was a year of greatness during Depression

For 1936, Chevrolet was doing well. This Master Deluxe coupe was a popular choice among Depression-era buyers.

Chevrolet was rolling from success to success by 1936, and little wonder. GM's lowest-priced car had become the darling of driveways across America due to value, motoring luxuries, improved ride and styling.

Automotively speaking, it wasn't easy to be a winner in 1936. The soured economy ravaged car company after car company from 1930 through 1935. In January of 1936, the Franklin plant at Syracuse, N.Y., sat quiet, the hum of progress having been halted by financial woes. There was a court contest with the city and a proposal to foreclose to the tune of an unpaid tax bill of $385,000. An entrepreneur in Detroit voiced his hope to purchase the plant.

Auburn concluded 1935 with a net loss of nearly $2.7 million. That was devastating news when coupled with the previous 1934 net loss of more than $3.6 million! Total assets for the whole operation by early 1936

This Master Deluxe coupe rolls on pressed-steel wheels, although wire wheels were optional. The right tail lamp and bumper guards were dealer-installed accessories.

were estimated at more than $3.8 million. The 1935 figure reflected a slip of nearly $2 million in assets. It spelled "the end."

Prosperous Chevrolet

Yet, optimism reigned at Chevrolet. Its firm position in the low-priced field meant that while higher-priced cars might topple from production heights and wane in memory, many buyers were abandoning that field in favor of medium-priced and low-priced offerings.

"Indications point to a good business year in 1936," said M.E. Coyle, who headed Chevrolet Motor Co. as general manager and president. His words were issued in early January of 1936. "Two significant facts indicate how our company regards the near future. We spent $25 million in plant expansion during 1935. The public has accepted our new models with an unprecedented enthusiasm that shows no abatement."

That was a 25 percent expansion. "A manufacturing company does not expand its production capacities by one-fourth unless it feels confident about the future," Coyle added. "The motoring public does not buy more than 180,000 Chevrolets in November and December unless there is need for new cars, buying capacity to purchase such quantities of large package merchandise and a confidence in continued economic improve-

For those who wanted an open Chevrolet in 1936, the company offered this Convertible Cabriolet. It was the only convertible in the Chevrolet stable that year.

ment. Barring unpredictable accidents, the progress made in 1935 should continue in the automobile industry. That industry is so large that as its forward movement continues, the effect produced upon all industry will be beneficial." He concluded with the observation that America had reclaimed its "former enterprising spirit, and this is a real basis for optimism."

In a survey of 23 states, the new 1936 Chevrolet was first in sales in all but three, with Ford running first in New Hampshire and North Dakota and Plymouth claiming top spot in Rhode Island. Overall, Ford consistently was running second, with Plymouth taking most of the third-place spots. Chevrolet was dominating the car markets in Pennsylvania, one of the biggest sales markets at the time. Chevrolet sales in that state alone for December of 1935 came to well over 23,000 units. This was a figure that would have meant potential salvation for Auburn or Franklin as a year-end total!

General Motors gambled on the future. There was no guarantee the economy would revive, and, in truth, there were more financial bumps to ride as the 1930s wound near conclusion. The optimism of GM executives was based on more than hopes or whims. There were facts. For 1935, GM overseas volume, for example, was nearly 29 percent ahead of 1934, and one analyst noted this marked "a full return to the levels prevailing in the peak years of 1928 and 1929." Plants were spinning out new GM cars not only in America but also Canada, England

Not very popular among buyers, the Convertible Cabriolet saw only 3,629 examples leave the factory in 1936.

and Germany. Sales of GM cars overseas were reflecting "substantial gains in practically all of the 104 countries comprising the overseas market," noted Chevrolet.

In America, Chevrolet was claiming 27 percent of the market, to Ford's 23-1/2 percent and Plymouth's nearly 14 percent. The aggregate total of the "Big Three" car makers (GM, Ford, Chrysler Corp.) was around 65 percent. Other car makers sliced up the remainder of the market.

Directing the dealers

Chevrolet did something else that proved very wise. Its executive field force was called to the main office in Detroit in late April of 1936. W. E. Holler, Chevrolet vice president and general sales manager, was in charge of the pep talk. Included in the huddle were nine regional managers, all 47 zone managers and 21 city managers. In all, personnel from Chevrolet's 10,000 dealers were represented by the executives.

Those dealers were to "reap maximum benefit from the elaborate sales machinery set up by Chevrolet," said Holler. "In anticipation of the greatest automotive market that has developed for several years, the company has gone ahead with several organization steps entirely new and unique. It has an en-

This four-door sedan wears dual sidemount spare tires. The option was a rare one and is seldom seen on 1936 Chevrolets.

tire department, with personnel throughout the United States, devoting all its time to the training of Chevrolet salesmen. Another whole department concentrates its attention on used cars, with highly gratifying results. The maintenance of a quality dealer body, with the right number of dealers in each community — each dealer properly located, staffed, and equipped — is the concern of still a third department. Dealer accounting and management occupies a fourth."

What Chevrolet officials realized was that the success of factories was directly equated with successful sales through a lively and healthy dealer organization. Without good outlets to buyer John Q. Public, Chevrolet factories would fall silent — as they did for Franklin and Auburn.

Knee-Action suspension and all-steel Turret Top construction were hallmarks of the 1936 Chevrolets. To trumpet these virtues to buyers, Chevrolet took to radio airwaves with its electrically transcribed program, "Musical Moments." Works from light musicals and popular tunes were sung and played with commercial plugs for Chevrolet interspersed between. The programs were produced under the auspices of Chevrolet and issued on 16-inch records, one 15-minute program per side. Local dealers were the conduit to stations, paying for air time as needed or leaning on friends for free time, if possible, when there was no competitor in town and the Chevrolet owner may have held a prominent position in local politics or social circles.

Safety affects sales

Increased output meant greater risk of injury among the factory work force. But with General Motors, that risk was greatly minimized for 1936. After all, injured workers meant delay, even sporadic shut-down of a line. It wasn't good for morale, either, let alone humanitarian concerns. For the first three months in 1936, the GM plants were reporting fewer accidents than any other similar period in company history. That was quite an achievement, since 74 plants were active in the United States and Canada. This included all types of accidents, and one reporter noted this indicated "that General Motors' workers are considerably safer at their work than they are on the streets or in their homes."

Specifically, in the first three months of 1936, there were only slightly less than five hours of lost time due to accidents for every million hours of work in GM plants. Impressive. This was an improvement of about 38 percent when compared to the same quarter in 1935. This was an even greater achievement when a substantial increase of work hours for 1936 was figured in.

With so many waves of success in 1936, Chevrolet was encouraging dealers to join their ranks in areas where new outlets were needed, by factory mandate. "When you have the Chevrolet franchise, you have friends," said the factory, sometimes running ads with this slogan bannered at the top and including a handshake blazoned inside the outline of the famous Chevrolet bow tie.

Dealers were encouraged to sign on, since their margin for profit was increased through the sale of trucks, too. "To the new series of Chevrolet passenger cars for 1936 — the only complete low-priced car — Chevrolet now adds a complete line of trucks and commercial cars, and thereby gives its dealers another great money-making opportunity," said officials.

"Chevrolet has made three major improvements in these new 1936 Chevrolet trucks: (1) It has increased power; (2) It has reduced operating costs to a new record low; and (3) it has modernized truck design and construction in every important part and feature. The proud result is America's most economical high-powered trucks — trucks which will be the first choice of alert business men — just as the new 1936 Chevrolet passengers cars are the first choice of the motoring public."

With so many successes going for Chevrolet in 1936, just imagine the smiles that must have resulted around the table of GM's executive board!

CHAPTER 5 | **1938 CHEVY COUPE BARN FIND**

By Brian Earnest

BACK FROM THE BARN
1938 Chevrolet Master Business Coupe was a long time coming

Richard Thomas' 1938 Chevy coupe is in a lot better shape today than it was about five years ago when he bought it (right). Thomas had known about the car for many years, and finally got the chance to own it after the car had been slumbering for many years in a farm shed.

Richard Thomas waited a long time to land his "Sweetie." More than four decades in fact. And when opportunity finally knocked, even at the least-expected time and most unlikely place, he didn't hesitate.

Thomas had known about the 1938 Chevrolet Master Business Coupe since he and the car's owner were childhood friends back in the 1960s. Even though he didn't own other collector cars and wasn't active in the car hobby, Thomas had always told his friend, Mike Webb, that he'd like to buy

22

his car someday. He was always rebuffed, until his luck finally began to change in late 2003. The two men bumped into each other at a garage sale after not seeing each other for many years, and Thomas again gave Webb his sales pitch. A year later, Thomas called him on the phone, still pining for the car. Then, finally, in December of 2004, the pair saw each other at another garage sale, and this time, Webb's tune had changed.

"I think he had hoped and hoped that he'd get around to restoring it, but his health was getting bad," said Thomas, a resident of Arkansas City, Kan. "Life isn't always fair, and it wasn't fair to him. He was having some hard times.

"But I was very surprised that he agreed to sell it to me. I could hardly believe it."

It would seem no great surprise that Webb would have trouble parting with the car he had owned for so many years. He had gotten the car from the original owner, Elijah Ham, who had purchased the car new from a fledgling dealership in Arkansas City. Ham, a friend of the Webb family, apparently drove the car very little, and during his retirement years decided to give the car to Mike Webb, who was just 14 at the time. Thomas says the other boys didn't know Webb even had such a car, but he remembers the day everyone found out!

"The first first time I saw it just a bunch of us guys 17, 18 years old, right in that area, we were just hanging out and doing what teenagers did in the '60s," he said. "I didn't even know he had it. I about died when I saw it. It was just a cool old car. Of course, we didn't really know much about it, I just thought it was cool.

"[He] let us all drool, then took it back to the house. He'd get it out on occasion. But he eventually had a little problem with the brakes — the positive battery cable rubbed a hole in the brake line. And one day he popped the brakes and ran into the back of a flatbed truck and put a nice crease in the grille. After that he rolled her into the barn and there she sat …

"It just stayed in the barn and as time went on, we both went our own ways and didn't much of each other. … Every once in a while we'd pass ways and I'd kind of half-heartedly say, "Hey, want to sell me that car yet?"

By the time Thomas got his chance to own the car, which he calls his "Sweetie," it had sat for more than 20 years. The gas had turned "to varnish" and the neglected Chevy was covered with a thick layer of dust. It had also become home to generations of unidentified varmints and various other creatures. It was a long way from the impressive, shiny coupe that Thomas remembered from his teenage years.

"I was kind of hoping it would be in that kind of shape where it had been setting for a while, but wasn't let go as much as it had been," he said. "I was hoping to change the oil, put a fresh battery in it and go for a ride. But that was not the case."

The term "barn find" is thrown around often in the old car hobby these days, but when Thomas found his forgotten '38 in a shed under a thick layer of dirt and surrounded by clutter, it was clear the car qualified.

The old Chevy was still structurally sound, but needed a lot of TLC, both inside and out. The old interior was in need of a lot of help.

Chevrolet's "diamond crown" styling changes were introduced for the 1937 models and carried over into 1938. The changes included safety glass in all the windows and fenders that were straight on the sides. The '38s had a new grille that alternated narrow and wide horizontal bars with a center molding down the middle. There were a few other styling tweaks for the '38s, but the body shells and running boards were the same on the '37s and '38s.

The hoods had ventilators with three chrome horizontal moldings. The headlamps were bullet-shaped and mounted close to the grille. Master series cars — there was also a higher-end Master Deluxe series — hand single tail lamps.

Under the hood was the familiar Chevy inline six, displacing 216.5 cubic inches and producing a modest 85 hp. A three-speed manual transmission with the stick on the floor was standard on all the bowtie '38s.

There were a total of 12 different Chevrolets available in 1938 — six each in both the Master and Master Deluxe lineups. The two-door town sedans were the most popular by far with 95,050 built, but coupes were also good sellers. A total of 39,793 coupes like Thomas' rolled off Chevy assembly lines carrying base prices of $648, which was the lowest MSRP on the Chevy menu.

Thomas began to bring his Sweetie back to life. He started by fixing the starter and fuel pump, but then made a costly mistake when he started the car without cleaning out the old gas tank.

"I finally did get it started. It ran — it was a little rough — but it did run," he recalls. "Well, after I got done bouncing off the walls with excitement, I took a couple of pictures of it running, then I shut it off and went inside. The next day I went out to start it again, it just went [insert loud engine noise sounds]! Come to find out the fresh gas I had put in it had melted enough varnish and the varnish had gotten up into the engine and stuck the valves shut. Overnight it had crystallized right in the engine. I had to buy a whole new set of push rods and whole set of lifters ... Now I preach that hard, hard: If you ever buy a car that hasn't been started in a long time, before you start it, pull the tank on it and clean it all out. You'll save yourself a lot of problems."

The next big step in what Thomas termed "a rolling restoration" was to replace much of the interior "so it didn't smell like a bathroom," he said. "I drove it that way for a while and actually took it to some shows. It was all pretty much original, except for the interior.

"Most of paint had popped off it. It had a lot of bare spots and lot of surface rust. I still had fun driving it and darn sure didn't have to worry about polishing it before went a show."

Thomas kept massaging the old '38 at a little at a time, fixing and replacing a few body panels, then priming the back half of the car and re-chroming the rear bumper. "From the side it looked kind of funny," he said. "The back half looked good and front half was all original."

Thomas eventually primed the front half of the car, too, and got the rest of the chrome done. "It had aftermarket fender shirts on it so it looked like a low-rider. It really looked cool!" he said.

The finishing touch finally came last winter when the car got a shiny new suit of black paint. "I decided to bite the bullet," Thomas said. The car is now arguably better than new, with options like fender skirts, heater, defroster, clock and ashtray that were not in the car when it was ordered new.

After waiting all these years, Thomas has no problems putting some miles on his Chevy, often with his wife Peggy riding shotgun. "She loves it and loves to go for rides," Thomas said. The coupe's odometer now reads 54,000-plus miles, and Thomas has accounted for about 6,000 of those. The Chevy's days of sitting sedentary in a barn appear to be long gone.

"It runs fine, it just doesn't run real fast," Thomas joked. "It's the old babbit-beater engine. It's basically the old oil-splash system. It will run forever as long as you don't over-rap it.

"I get it out when the weather is good. I try to drive it at least once a week. I run across people who'll see the car and say, 'Hey, I remember when Mike's mom used to drive that car.' Some of the old-timers around here remember it."

CHAPTER 6 | 1941 CABRIOLET
By Jerry Didonato

RELIVING YESTERDAY IN A '41 CABRIOLET

Jerry Didonato bought this 1941 Chevrolet Cabriolet in 1946 at the age of 17 (left). He and his wife purchased his current '41 in 1979 and then restored it.

I was born in Webster, Mass., on Sept. 10, 1929, as one of eight children, and the youngest of five boys. Our beginnings were humble, partly because my parents were immigrants, and partly because it was at the start of the Depression. We earned what we received; hard work was the name of the game back then. Like most young boys, I was fascinated by cars. My older bothers had their own cars, and it seemed like a faraway dream to me. I realized my dream in 1946 at the age of 17.

The car I purchased was a 1941 Chevrolet Cabriolet. I courted Pauline in that car

26

and later, at 19, we married. We enjoyed the Chevrolet for a long time, traveling the Mohawk Trail, among other places. When our son was born, we needed something enclosed, but we still had hopes of purchasing another 1941 Chevrolet someday to bring back the memories of our first car. That dream came true in 1979, when we found the same model of Chevrolet. We were excited with our purchase, because we were able to keep the promise we had made to ourselves in the early 1950s.

The 1941 Chevrolet Cabriolet we purchased in 1979 is green with a six-cylinder, 216-hp engine with overhead valves. It also has a three-speed manual transmission with vacuum shift and big whitewall tires. The restoration was very costly, considering that my first car cost $800, a price I met with some help from Dad. Also, this car was spending most of its time in the garage, but I found that restoring it became a labor of love. Since then, I have spent a great deal of money on restoring many items. As an example, a radio that cost $64.50 in 1941 was $1,500 to replace; a built-in spinner in the steering wheel originally cost $12.50 back then, now cost $1,500 as a replacement; a compass of the era cost $2.95 and $1,000 at the time of restoration; a $7 umbrella holder cost $500 during the restoration. But the love of the car and the memories it evoked were worth all the time, money and effort.

My wife was so supportive that, when she read an ad in a newspaper about a car show in nearby Shirley, Mass., she encouraged me to enter. I did, and won first place. I became hooked on car shows and entered just about every show possible. I also joined the Antique Automobile Club of America (AACA). Later on, Pauline accompanied me to many car shows.

The first year I entered the AACA show in Hershey, Pa., was 1991. I won a First Junior award that year and a First Senior the second year, followed by Preservation Awards in subsequent years. In 2002, my car was chosen for the Grand National Award in Philadelphia. I have continued to enter AACA shows and the car has won all the awards a car can win. To date, I have 35 AACA Preservation Awards and 9 Grand National Awards, plus many other local and special awards.

In part, I owe a debt of gratitude to Old Cars Weekly, which listed many of the parts I needed for sale.

Unfortunately, Pauline died of cancer in 1995. She really started the ball rolling on car shows, and to perpetuate her memory, I sponsor the Pauline Didonato Award through the Webster-Dudley Lions Club. Yearly, they hold an end-of-the-year blowout and they pay tribute to her memory by this award. It is an award given to a car, truck or motorcycle that I select, based on the type of vehicle I think Pauline would like. It was her support that has allowed me to enter and win so many awards.

CHAPTER 7 | ***1941 OPTIONS***

Story and photos by Dan Burrill

50 REASONS TO LOVE A '41 CHEVROLET

Fender skirts, a "flying lady" hood ornament, fender "washboards," spotlights, and boot scrapers along the rocker panels are just some of the accessories on this fully loaded 1941 Chevrolet Cabriolet.

Today's cars come with many standard features that were rare options 60 years ago. This perfectly restored 1941 Chevrolet Cabriolet, owned by Ron Wade, is a classic example of the rare options available on a Chevrolet before World War II. In fact, this car is so unusual and so well restored that it won the prestigious Vintage Chevrolet Club of America's Best of Show. But the really unusual things about this car are the 50 factory-offered options or accessories that are on it.

Ron Wade is responsible for joining all of the options and accessories on the show-winning 1941 Chevrolet pictured here.

Wade is a visionary when it comes to rare and collectable cars. In the early 1970s, he put together a list of the 25 most desirable

The left and right spotlights with the ivory ball on the handle were only offered for the first half of the model year.

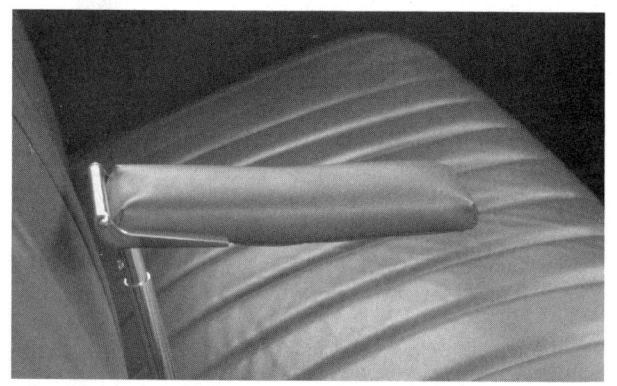

Center armrest. This center armrest was an unusual item that adds a nice touch to the burgundy front seat.

Town and Country horn on the instrument panel.

cars he would like to own. The cars on his list were low-production, high-performance, convertible models or luxury cars.

At the time he put the list together, Wade didn't own any of these cars and, in some cases, it would be years before he actually found the cars and started restoring them. However, he knew what he wanted and started buying NOS parts and accessories for them while they were still available at swap meets and from dealers. Years later, when he actually started restoring the low-production collector cars on his list, he already had a stockpile of parts.

One of those cars high on Wade's wish list was a 1941 Chevrolet Cabriolet, such as the car pictured here, so he bought '41 Chevrolet parts whenever he could. In 1984, he bought his first '41 Chevrolet Cabriolet, and before he started restoring it, folks came by with a better car that they were going to ship to Australia. But when they discovered the cost to ship a car

Super Deluxe heater and the defroster are two items that we think of as being part of any modern car, but the defroster and the Super Deluxe Heater were options in 1941. The optional under-seat heater couldn't be used with the Cabriolet, because there was an X-member added to the frame for additional support.

that far, they opted to trade the car to Wade for a crate of original vintage Chevrolet parts, which were shipped in place of the car, and at a lower rate. In the trade, Wade received a nicer car to restore.

Although Wade had many of the required optional accessories, there were many more that are so rare it took years to acquire. In fact, several of the accessories on this car may very well be the only ones left in existence.

When talking about this car, the word "rare" comes up about 100 times in the conversation. In fact, it took Ron years just to find the books, brochures and part catalogs that showed pictures of some of the original accessories. From these sources, the search was on for the actual items.

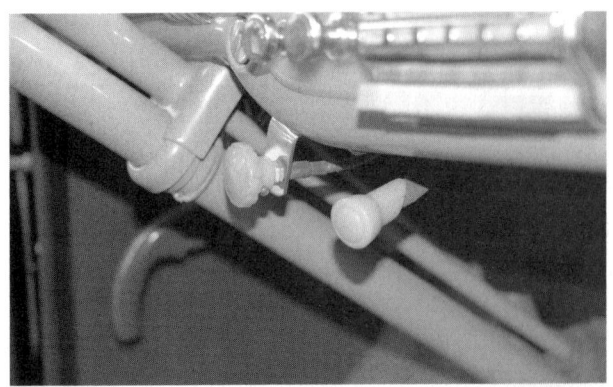

Ivory cowl vent knob.

The "shark's tail" exhaust tip is extremely rare. Also note the bumper extensions (wings).

30

Radiator overflow return tank on the passenger side of the firewall.

Fold-down rear bumper guard. The rear guard had to fold down for the spare tire to be removed.

The windshield washer reservoir bottle with pump on the right side of firewall.

Needless to say, this is a body-off-frame restoration that took years to complete. The car was in average condition for a '41, so once the car was completely dismantled, everything required cleaning, fixing, re-welding, reinforcement or replacement.

Like all restored vehicles, the work was tremendous and very time consuming. The restoration was done by Bill Baker; the paint and body by Keith Grendahl at New

Electric clock. The gold in the electric clock is a different color than the gold in the speedometer, even though they were from the same year.

Start Autobody; upholstery by the late Ken Jones; and a great deal of credit goes to master technician Ray Holland for his help in finishing the project.

After years of collecting parts, Wade's passion finally developed into a business and for the last 26 years his company, Chevs of the 40's in Vancouver, Wash., has been providing the best in restoration parts for 1937-'54 Chevrolet Cars and Trucks. And, of course, the "Fabulous '41," has become the flagship car for the company.

On these pages are some of the 50 original accessories that make this a very rare car.

CHAPTER 8 — 1949 CHEVY KICK-OFF
By Phil Hall

1949 NEW-CAR INTRODUCTION WAS A FAMILY AFFAIR

A crowd of spectators and potential buyers jam a showroom at a dealership in Milwaukee, Wis. in January of 1949 to look at an all-new 1949 Chevy DeLuxe Styleline convertible. Such gatherings at the time became neighborhood social events. (Phil Hall collection)

It was a neighborhood social event. It was something the dreams of young boys (and not-so-young boys) were made of. It was looked forward to with great anticipation. It was even something to get dressed up for.

What could garner all this attention? Why, the introduction of the new models at the local automobile dealership, of course. A rite of fall (most of the time), just like the changing leaves, was the first showing of the coming model year's cars, and, to a lesser extent, trucks.

Today, with new vehicle introductions virtually year around, and with so many different makes and models getting new designs and model-year designations seemingly at random, the annual big introductions are all but forgotten. You can see new models well ahead of their showroom appearances at auto shows, on television, on the internet, and in countless publications. So, by the time the vehicles reach the dealers, their styling, features, and new gimmicks are already well known. Also, the dealership is less likely to be close to home, as one has to go to the mega dealers on auto row or the auto mall.

However, for some of us, fond memories of the new model-year debuts at showrooms can be savored. For this writer, a walk with the family to a nearby Chevrolet dealer to see the 1950 models on introduction night was priceless, as they say.

The showroom was full of new cars (well, three anyway) and people, several of whom were well-known locally. The walk back home and the night were spent pondering how neat it would be to have a new Chevrolet, even though the family at the time didn't have a car and didn't have the money to buy one, new or otherwise. Someday…

While the changes between the 1950 and 1949 Chevrolets were minimal (each duly noted by this young spectator), that introduction fell into the timeframe of excitement among new car buyers. Indeed, the new postwar styling, which came make by make in the late 1940s, was coupled with increased availability, as postwar waiting lists dried up and new cars could be purchased from dealer stock or ordered from the factory and delivered within weeks rather than years.

These newly designed cars were refreshing glimpses into the future, after years of the prewar and warmed-over versions thereof.

Studebaker and Kaiser-Frazer got us going in 1947 with new designs. Hudson, Oldsmobile 98, and Cadillac followed for 1948. In mid 1948, Ford brought out the really new 1949 Ford. For 1949, it became a deluge with the rest of General Motors (except the Cadillac 75), Mercury, Lincoln, Nash, and, after late start, Chrysler Corp. all bringing out all-new cars. Each introduction ensured a crowded showroom of lookers and potential buyers.

Today, import brands have gobbled up more than half of the new-car market, but in the late 1940s, domestic brands were the show … period. Only fringe buyers looked at imports, and for them, the new-model introduction and model-year changes were all but unknown.

Chevrolet for 1949 was among the all-new cars for that model year. Introduction came early in 1949, about six months after Ford, but still a few ahead of rival Plymouth. Like the other Mopar brands, Plymouth had to start the 1949 model year with first-series cars, which were part of an extended run of 1948 models.

The 1949 Chevrolets looked much sleeker

To show off what was under the all-new Chevrolet styling for 1949, this display traveled around the country to auto shows and other public events. Other manufacturers also pulled out all the stops to sell their new vehicles. (Phil Hall collection)

than the 1948 models and were inches lower in overall height. Wheelbase length was shortly less at 115 inches, and overall length (except wagons) was close to the 1948 figure at 197 or so inches. Replacing the 1948's standard 16-inch wheels were 15-inchers. For 1948, 15-inch wheels were optional.

For 1949, there were two series (DeLuxe and Special), and within the series, there were Fleetline (fastback sedans) and Styleline (notchback) sedans, coupes, and convertibles. Styleine wagons at first came with either all-steel or part-wood construction.

The 90-hp, 216.5-cid, overhead-valve six was probably the least-changed major component on the 1949 Chevrolet. New features all helped Chevrolet model-year production to 1,037,600, well above the 715,992 of the 1948 models. However, the little-changed 1950 models would do even better at 1,371,535.

The basic 1949 styling continued through the 1952 model year. It was altered for 1953 and 1954, before the all-new 1955 models took Chevrolet down several new paths.

The phenomenon of the new-model showroom big event would continue for many years, but with diminishing effect. Perhaps the late-1940s introductions of all-new postwar models were the high point. You had to have been there to understand if it was.

CHAPTER 9 | **1953 BEL AIR WAGON**

By Angelo Van Bogart

A DANDY FOR DINAH

Dinah Shore had her own one-of-a-kind 1953 Bel Air wagon

This 1953 Chevrolet Bel Air station wagon was styled for Dinah Shore. The unique car's features included a 1950 hood ornament (top left), a musical bar emblem with Shore's initials "ds" on the door beneath the beltline (right) and two-toning, plus many other features. (General Motors LLC photos)

Dinah Shore didn't just sing the virtues of Chevrolet, she experienced them.

Shore's connection with Chevrolet goes back to at least the early 1950s, when her show was sponsored by the automaker. "The Dinah Shore Show" was launched in 1951, and by at least 1953, Shore was singing what would become her trademark tune,

"See the U.S.A. in your Chevrolet:"

"See the U.S.A.
in your Chevrolet
America is asking you to call.
Drive your Chevrolet,
through the U.S.A.
America's the greatest land of all.

36

The horn button reads, "Styled for Dinah Shore." (General Motors LLC photo)

On a highway or a road along a levee,
performance is sweeter,
nothing can beat 'er,
life is completer in a Chevy!
So make a date today,
to see the U.S.A,
and see it in your Chevrolet.

This tune, sung on television by Shore over many years, became so popular, the star became known for her connection with the "bow tie" brand. Aiding this was the move to rename Shore's program "The Dinah Shore Chevy Show" from 1957 to 1961.

Perhaps as a "thank you" measure in June 1953, a special Chevrolet was created for Shore — a 1953 Chevrolet Bel Air station wagon decked with a "ds" badge on the door, a steering wheel horn button stating the car was "Styled for Dinah Shore" and many other unusual features, leaving no doubt for whom it was built.

The Bel Air name had only been used on Chevrolet's top-line hardtop from 1950-'52. In 1953, use of the Bel Air name expanded to a full series when it became Chevrolet's top-of-the-line model to include a convertible, sedan, coupe and, of course, a hardtop. Not included in this series was a station wagon, which was added for the 1954 model year. Instead, the company's three 1953 station wagons were comprised of two mid-level Two-Ten models and a single model in the base One-Fifty line.

The One-Fifty Handyman wagon was Chevrolet's entry-level station wagon in 1953. It seated six people and had a folding rear seat. Like the rest of the One-Fifty series, it featured very little decorative trim and was a no-nonsense people (or cargo) hauler.

The Two-Ten series also had a six-passenger Handyman station wagon with a folding rear seat. However, it was trimmed better than the One-Fifty inside and out with standard Two-Ten exterior trim.

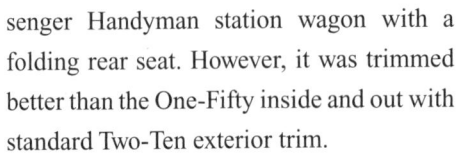

The top-of-the-line Two-Ten Townsman station wagon featured simulated wood-grain trim beneath the side windows and at the beltline, as well as on the tailgate. It also upped the Handyman wagons of the Two-Ten and One-Fifty series by providing seating for eight passengers. Had a Bel Air station wagon been offered, it would have been the Townsman station wagon. However, this wagon's exterior clearly used Two-Ten exterior trim, leaving no doubt to its place in the Chevrolet line.

Since Shore was a one-of-a-kind herself, Chevrolet must have seen fit to give her a one-of-a-kind vehicle. That vehicle was the Bel Air-trimmed station wagon shown here. Inside and out, Shore's unique 1953 Bel Air received many appointments that differentiated it from a Two-Ten. All that is known to remain of that car are the vintage photographs shown here, supplied by Vintage Chevrolet Club of America member and OCW subscriber Bruce Granger and the GM Media Archives.

On the outside, Shore's Bel Air station

Above: The rear fenders of Shore's Chevrolet received Bel Air trim, unique placement for the "Bel Air" name and a cane work-type pattern in the space between the horizontal stainless trim pieces. Right: Shore's Chevrolet had a unique, externally mounted spare with a wheel center stamped with "Bel Air." (General Motors LLC photos)

wagon received a unique two-tone paint treatment that included a contrasting color to the lower portion of the doors and front fender to match the roof. The car appears to lack the woodgrain pattern on the beltline and tailgate of top-line Two-Ten Townsman station wagons (and 1954 Bel Air station wagons). Meanwhile, the headlamp bezels of Shore's car appear to be contemporary Cadillac units, with the hooded portion of the bezel painted the station wagon's main body color. Although two hood ornaments were offered in 1953, Shore's car sports neither. The stylized bird hood ornament is actually a deluxe accessory 1950 Chevrolet part. The Chevrolet "bow tie" on each of the unique wagon's Bel Air hubcaps also appears to be painted a lighter color, possibly the body color, rather than the standard dark blue. Finally, and most importantly, the car sports Bel Air trim on the rear doors and fenders, with a unique treatment to the area between the parallel-running stainless Bel Air trim pieces. The treatment in this area of the rear fender may be painted or a special trim insert, and regardless, it's not a treatment found on any other Bel Air.

Oddly, the "Bel Air" emblem does not appear between the horizontal stainless trim pieces on the rear fenders as on other 1953

Bel Air models. Instead, it's located just in front of the tail lamp on the side of the rear fender.

At the tailgate, the station wagon incorporated a unique-for-Chevrolet spare tire with an equally one-off spare tire center stamped with the "Bel Air name."

Photos show the inside of this unique station wagon has door panels with a vertically ribbed pattern more in line with Bel Air models, and certainly of a different pattern and configuration of Two-Ten Townsman station wagons. In addition, the seat upholstery has vertical pleats in a style more like the Bel Air than the Two-Ten sedan. Furthermore, the window frames appear in the black-and-white images to be chrome-plated. And, of course, there's that special "Styled for Dinah Shore" horn button.

The number of Chevrolets Shore sold by promoting them on her program cannot be counted, but Shore's touting of its virtues with the catchy jingle still resonate today. However, the whereabouts of this single Bel Air station wagon remain a mystery. Granger and OCW would love to know the fate of this vehicle. Anyone with information is asked to write or e-mail OCW at angelo.vanbogart@ fwmedia.com.

Author's note: The author is indebted to Bruce Granger for bringing this car to our attention and supplying leads to the images here, as well as Chevrolet expert Kenny Buttolph for providing his insight.

CHAPTER 10 — 1953 STEPVAN

Story and photos by Chad Elmore

STEP UP TO THE COOL-AS-ICE CREAM BIG BAR STEPVAN

The Kent's Big Bar 1953 Chevrolet stepvan is a hit at car events, and on the street.

By restoring and utilizing old vehicles, hobbyists are keeping history alive. There's another reason, too: most old cars and trucks are simply fun to drive, and you can't beat the attention they draw. But you're not likely to see a 50-some-year-old delivery truck undergo a much-needed restoration unless its owner can put it back on the payroll.

Most bread and milk trucks were scrapped once their useful lives ran out. Tom and Kathy Truhlar have the perfect application for such an antique, and they did not let a former bread truck get away.

The Truhlars are the owners of Kent's Ice Cream, a registered dairy plant in Fort Atkinson, Wis.; their Big Bar ice cream bars are popular treats at old car shows, vintage

41

tractor meets and flea markets throughout Illinois and Wisconsin. Tom and Kathy's freshly restored Kent's Ice Cream 1953 Chevrolet stepvan made its debut at the 2005 Spring Jefferson swap meet in Jefferson, Wis., six miles north of Fort Atkinson. "It was a hit," said Tom. "Many people came up and said, 'Those used to be on the road all the time years ago when I was a kid, but I haven't seen one since.'"

Kent's Ice Cream was founded in Fort Atkinson in 1941, and its retail store was a popular hangout into the 1970s. Scooping ice cream eventually evolved into the more portable Big Bar, which was — as it is today — made by hand from original recipes. The retail store was closed in favor of selling the treats exclusively at local events, and that's still the best place to find them. The Truhlars purchased the dairy business in 1999, then moved to Fort Atkinson from Michigan's Upper Peninsula.

For many hobbyists, buying a Big Bar at an old-car

The Chevy had been used to deliver bread and later vend plants by "The Plant Pedlar." By the time Tom and Kathy Truhlar saw the stepvan, it had been parked for a couple decades and was looking rather tired.

Above, Truhlar rewired the truck and replaced the wood in the dashboard. Right, Removing the covers makes getting to the 235-cid engine and its updraft Carter carburetor relatively easy.

event is one tradition that does not get broken, regardless of weather. During the upper Midwest's colder months, it's not unusual to see people wearing gloves and heavy jackets lined up at the vending window for one of eight Big Bar varieties (the sunflower seed-coated, chocolate-covered vanilla bar is the most popular, but you've got to try the new grape sorbet, as well).

That's exactly how the Truhlars were introduced to the approximately frozen treats. "During the winter in Michigan's U.P., you need a hobby," said Tom. "We turned to restoring an old car every winter." The Truhlars' restoration projects included their own 1966 Pontiac LeMans two-door hardtop, and a rare 1969 Buick GS400 Stage 1 convertible owned by a friend.

"Our favorite swap meets for finding parts included the spring and fall Jefferson events," said Tom. "We would each have three Big Bars a day and consider that lunch, as we couldn't get them anywhere else."

The Truhlars often sell the Big Bars in several locations at one show, or participate in two different events on the same weekend. This requires some help from friends and a small fleet of trucks and freezer-equipped vending trailers.

In April 2004, a friend, a retired mechanic, told the Truhlars about an old stepvan that was for sale. He had worked on the aging truck when it was used for selling plants at a local farmer's market. For Tom and Kathy, seeing the truck in person didn't equate to love at first sight. "It had sat for a few decades behind a building in Stoughton, Wis.," Tom said. "The stepvan was a storage shed for car parts, mice and hornets. The large front window's southern exposure created a greenhouse for grape vines and blackberry bushes, which had overtaken the Spartan cab."

The vehicle was in sad shape, but the Grumman body was aluminum (no rust!) and fairly straight. The Truhlars thought about the truck for several days before visiting it again. "We began to think about its potential use for our business," said Tom. "We needed another vending truck to carry freezers. And the fact the owner had installed $400 worth of new tires and the asking price was $500 made it seem like a better deal."

The truck was hauled home, and Tom began digging into the mechanicals. Most of the parts are shared with the 1947-'53 Chevy 3/4-ton pickup and were easy to locate. Finding other pieces (such as the special intake/exhaust manifold and updraft carburetor setup used on Chevy's forward-control and cab-over trucks) required walking swap meets and a little luck. While traveling along a Wisconsin back road, Tom spotted a similar Grumman body on a Ford chassis. After weeks of negotiating with the Ford's owner, the Chevrolet stepvan had a parts donor. The Grumman body's unique curved corner windshield pieces, both of which had taken bullets in the Chevy, were

Above, Tom Truhlar does a little body work after 1,100 lbs. of baking soda were use to clean the aluminum body. Right, Rick Foley, from Sodaworks, used 1,100 lbs. of baking soda to clean the aluminum body.

removed first. The rest of the stepvan's windows used flat glass, which was easily replaced.

The Grumman Corp. had made a name for itself during World War II, but it wasn't by building bread trucks. Grumman was the Navy's primary aircraft manufacturer. After the war, with increased competition for lucrative military contracts, Grumman started diversifying its product offering. While civilian aircraft and crop-dusters were a natural extension, it also began using its expertise with aluminum to make products, such as canoes and delivery truck bodies.

Grumman's involvement with trucks began in 1946. Jimmy Olson and Walter Heingartner founded a company to sell trucks to the laundry industry. Grumman co-founder Jack Sirbul, who was one of Olson's friends, was convinced to build the bodies at Grumman. In 1948, Grumman and Olson developed the aluminum Kurbside walk-in body, which was placed on a modified Chevrolet chassis. Over the years, the Grumman Olson company picked up lucrative contracts to build trucks for the United States Postal Service and UPS, but by the turn of the current century, Grumman Olson was in trouble. The stepvan business found new owners in 2003, and is now operating under the Morgan Olson brand.

The Truhlars' Grumman-bodied 1953 stepvan was made roadworthy by rebuilding the original 235-cid engine and four-speed manual transmission. A complete brake rebuild was also performed. The truck's original 5.14 rear was replaced when a 1963 Chevrolet 3/4-ton Camper Special pickup donated its 4.56 rear.

"It will go 50 mph now," said Tom, "but the original top-end speed had to be around 35 mph with the stock gears."

The delivery truck was driven to a cruise-in in Fort Atkinson in mid-August 2004. Parked next to the original Kent's Big Bar hauler (a clean, slightly modified three-door 1972 Chevrolet Suburban), a sign on the stepvan provided passers-by with a vision of what the truck would look like once Spring Jefferson — generally considered the start of old-car season in Wisconsin — rolled around a mere eight months later.

After the cruise, the real work began on the body. The Truhlars' plan from the beginning was to give the stepvan a working-class restoration. "We want people to enjoy the truck. At Jefferson, several people used the front bumper as a bench to take a break and enjoy a Big Bar," said Tom. "We didn't want to worry about that at shows."

Body modifications included cutting in a selling window and a roof vent, while repairs required filling more than 50 holes where signs and shelves had once been bolted, and hand-forming a new rear door.

Removing layers of old paint and the "Plant Pedlar" signage without warping the aluminum skin was done by Rick Foley from Sodaworks in Highland, Wis. Foley's mobile baking soda paint removal unit arrived in Fort Atkinson in late October. Foley worked 7 1/2 hours and used 1,100 lbs. of baking soda to make the truck's body look like the inside of a soda can.

To take care of any aluminum oxidation in the stepvan's cavernous interior, Tom and Kathy polished and buffed the inside panels to shine them up.

Tom painted the body in a friend's paint booth, giving it a tri-color treatment to keep the 1950s theme. The roof is white over a 1960 Ford light green body with accents painted a dark Oliver tractor green.

Within a couple months of the Spring Jefferson swap meet, the Truhlars had made a remarkable amount of progress. The truck had been wired to accept three large ice cream freezers, and the dashboard was rebuilt. But no deadline is complete without a few late nights. "A week before the show, we finally finished it up and put on graphics with a 1950s theme," said Tom. "Then, with two days to spare, the truck was complete."

For now, Tom and Kathy plan to use the stepvan at events within an hour of Fort Atkinson, or where interstate travel is not required. "We'll keep pushing it a little farther as we get more comfortable with the truck," said Tom. "It was not made to go too fast, so I love the shows we can attend by using the back roads." (Check their website at www.kentsbigbar.com for updates).

Big Bar devotees will tell you it's difficult to stop at just one or two, and it's a challenge many car collectors are faced with, as well. The Truhlars are no different: they've already added another unique vehicle to the Kent's Ice Cream fleet. While visiting the Chickasha Swap Meet in Chickasha, Oklahoma, in May of 2005, they spotted a rust-free 1961 International one-ton truck. "The potential with the International truck is so sweet, we really couldn't pass it up," said Tom. "We have an old frozen pizza delivery body on a late-model diesel Ford chassis, which we put 74 miles on last year. That's not cost-effective with a diesel."

Tom is still investigating what job the dually International Harvester truck originally performed, but it came from an air base where it apparently did a lot of stationary work. It's fitted with an extra-large radiator, and the odometer shows less than 4,000 miles. The plan is to transfer the freezer body to the International, and the search for restoration parts has already begun.

Tom said the Big Bar stepvan took a little more money than they had originally planned on, but it is already paying off with valuable exposure and more sales. "The Suburban was always nice at shows," said Tom, "but it is not the same as having something really old and unique like the stepvan. Car hobbyists understand."

CHAPTER 11 — 1955 BISCAYNE SHOW CAR
By Angelo Van Bogart

CHEVROLET DREAM CAR'S PIECES COME BACK TOGETHER

The 1955 Biscayne show car as it appeared before the public at Motorama displays throughout the country. Dream car collector Joe Bortz considers this car to be a "beautiful Level 1" dream car, because it is a completely original, one-of-a-kind show car sharing no body components with production cars.

Resurrecting the 1955 Chevrolet *Biscayne* show car isn't quite like Johnny Cash's song about assembling a Cadillac with parts from the assembly line; it's more like assembling a 1,000-piece puzzle with many of the pieces missing.

Since saving the tattered and scattered remains of the ex-General Motors show car more than a decade ago from dream car goldmine Warhoop's Used Auto and Truck Parts in Warren, Mich., owner Joe Bortz and his restoration team completed significant amounts of work to the body of the Biscayne and expected its restoration to be finished in July 2010.

"When I (first) saw the Biscayne, it was just a body

47

The Biscayne as it appeared when Bortz first saw it at Warhoop's Used Auto and Truck Parts in 1989. The car is seen in its cut-up state with the doors and roof severed, but the lower half was uncut. (Joe Bortz photo)

with no doors on it," Bortz said. "The roof was laying inside the car and the doors were inside the car. It was just a total wreck. If you would have looked at it, you would have said there's no way anybody is going to salvage this.

"It was just piled up, laying on top of a bunch of cars in a corner (of the yard) where you couldn't see it." But after years of work, the Biscayne's future is looking much brighter.

"The body really looks terrific, and we are preparing a chassis for this project, which we expect to have finished by the summer of 2004," Bortz said in an interview in January of that year.

Even though the Biscayne had seen little or no road action, Bortz' crew had to dedicate a significant amount of work to its body, because the car had been cut into 10 pieces by yard owner Harry Warhoop Sr. to fulfill GM's mandate that the car be destroyed shortly after arriving at his yard. After cutting the Biscayne into pieces, Warhoop scattered its various body sections throughout the yard, often hiding parts in other vehicles rusting away on the property.

"The story goes that two days before

A member of the restoration crew, "John B.," leans against the reassembled body of the Biscayne. Parts of the original light metallic green paint are still visible on the car. The car's chassis will be finished by the summer of 2004. (Joe Bortz photo)

Christmas, they (General Motors) sent one of their people to Warhoop's with two of the cars, the LaSalle II roadster and the Biscayne," Bortz relates. "They were smart enough not to send the car over to the junkyard and say, 'crush this car.' They sent one of their people to give witness to the cutting of the car and then the crushing," Bortz said.

"The guy was supposed to sit there and watch [the show cars] get cut and then crushed. So they took the cars, the LaSalle II and the Biscayne, and they cut them. They cut the doors off, the roof off (of the cars)." Having witnessed the cutting of the cars, Bortz was told the GM representative said, "I know you guys will do it. Just put it in the crusher. I want to get home." When the GM representative left, Warhoop took the pieces and hid them, knowing he was preserving history for the future.

"The next day, the day before Christmas Eve, [GM] brought in the other two cars, the LaSalle II sedan and the '56 Caddy Eldorado Brougham Town Car, and [the GM representative] said, 'I can't wait around for you guys to cut them up. Just cut 'em up, crush 'em, and I'll just mark down that

I saw everything.' So they took these two cars complete and hid them." This related story explains why Bortz found the LaSalle II roadster and the Biscayne cut into pieces, but mostly complete, and both the Eldorado Brougham Town Car and LaSalle II sedan complete and uncut. When Warhoop's eventually offered the cars to Bortz, he purchased all four.

GM may have originally trusted Warhoop's to crush the cars, but the company inadvertently wound up trusting the yard to preserve its past.

In a Nov. 23, 1989, Old Cars Weekly article that appeared shortly after Bortz found the cars, Bortz said that while the cars were cut apart, their dismemberment by Warhoop's had been carefully done so as to keep their components from being destroyed.

"They (the parts) were cut up and distributed throughout the yard," Bortz said in that 1989 article. "One (Warhoop's) employee found the top of the Biscayne in a panel truck. It was like getting a Renwal model car kit, but it was a real car."

Warhoop's was so careful in keeping parts of the show cars they had disassembled so many years earlier that when it came time to dig out a chrome generator for one of the LaSalle II's Bortz had bought, Warhoop remembered, after some careful thought, that it had been stashed behind a rafter in his shop.

When found, the Biscayne lacked a chassis, so Bortz' restoration crew constructed a new chassis from a production 1955 Chevrolet frame.

"The chassis is a '55 Chevy chassis at the front and then it narrows down to accommodate this body," Bortz said. "Right now, we're in the process of taking the '55 Chevy chassis and making it fit the rest of the body, and then we can start the restoration of it." Unlike the rear, the front of the production frame will require little, if any, modification.

"Internationally known rod and custom fabricator Kerry Hopperstead is making up the chassis, and after that, we'll get into the actual restoration." A correct-for-1955 small-block 265-cid V-8 and Powerglide transmission was matched to the chassis, just as Chevrolet had originally installed in the Biscayne's engine bay.

In 2004, Bortz has the fiber glass-bodied Biscayne's body to the point where the doors swing open and the roof is back on.

"We worked on it for a couple of years and got the whole body together, so it is now ready to drop on a chassis," Bortz said at that time.

Bortz also has the original windshield for the car, but it's cracked beyond repair. It did, however, provide a template for a new piece of glass.

The car is "amazingly complete, but there are always things you have to make," Bortz said. "That's just part of getting into these really, really high-tech, high-dollar-cost restorations."

Joe Bortz recently added the 1961 Pontiac Monte Carlo to his collection of dream cars.

Because it had been dissected, the Biscayne had its share of parts that needed to be handmade. "There were a few trim parts missing that we're going to have to make, but a lot of the important trim pieces, like the trim on the front and the headlight bezels, were still on the car." Some of those parts were made in-house, but sometimes they were farmed out to fabricators or done in collaboration with Bortz' team and outside fabricators. Such restoration tasks require time. Not wanting to show the Biscayne until after it was finished, Bortz displayed the car in its unrestored (but assembled) condition at the 2008 Pebble Beach Concours d'Elegance, a first for a car that direly needed to be resurrected. It was joined by other restored and unrestored dream cars from his collection, including the Wildcat I, LaSalle roadster and Bonneville coupe.

Bortz enjoys sharing his collection. Before 2008, the last time his cavalcade of dream cars toured venues throughout the United States was in the early 1990s. But keep your eyes open — you might just spot the Biscayne roll into a show near you.

He's also not done looking for retired dream cars. The latest addition to his collection is the acquisition of the 1961 Pontiac Monte Carlo, an open two-seater based on a shortened-chassis Tempest with a wraparound cockpit windscreen. Like so many other Motorama dream cars, the Monte Carlo had found itself in good hands.

CHAPTER 12 | **1955 BEL AIR SEDAN**

By Brian Earnest

FOUR-DOOR DREAM
Florida hobbyist stumbles upon pristine '55 Bel Air sedan that's as original as they come

Except for the water pump, four new tires and some belts and hoses, Don Pardo's 17,000-mile 1955 Bel Air sedan has not changed since the day it rolled out of the factory

There are plenty old car hobby folks around who don't get too excited about a four-door sedan. It doesn't really matter the make, model or year, they simply don't find much animal attraction to anything with more than two doors.

Don Pardo isn't one of those guys.

Pardo insists he likes the sedans just as much as he likes the two-door coupes and convertibles. In fact, the Brooksville, Fla., resident was looking specifically for a humble sedan during a trip back to his old stomping grounds in Indiana back in 2006. He found one alright — a shockingly original 1955 Chevrolet Bel Air with just 14,000 miles.

Pardo's dilemma these days is that the two-tone green Chevy is so pristine and such a time capsule that he is afraid to drive it.

"Well, the first thing I did when I got it

was jump in it and take it across the Ohio state line to a show," said Pardo. "I planned to drive it. Well, the people there couldn't believe it. They all said, "Well, I didn't know about that car. If I would have known about it, I would have tried to buy it.' But the car had been for sale, and none of them had even gone to look at it.

"Well, when we got home later, I had a friend from Super Chevy come and look at it, and before he even started looking at the numbers and stuff, he said, 'Do you know what it would cost to restore this car.' He was amazed. He scared me into not driving it.

"Now, I'm afraid to have any fun with it, and it's no fun having it sit it a corner say-ing, 'I've got this.' It really needs to be in a museum, or a collection somewhere where people can see it. I really wish I could find a dealer that would buy it and it and put it up as a display piece in their showroom."

Pardo isn't totally clear on why the car was so lightly used by its first owner, other than the fact that the man was a fuel oil delivery man for many years and apparently opted to drive his work truck a lot more than his Bel Air. When the original owner died, the car wound up with his son, who kept in it a clean, dry storage barn until Pardo stumbled upon the car and bought it. Somehow, the car had been run just enough to keep it from getting too crusty. Clearly, however, it had never been much of a daily driver.

"No, I don't think it ever just sat," he said. "They took care of it, but I'm not sure what they did. It was like this when I first saw it. I turned the key and drove it home!

"My brother knew this man's dad. I had called him and asked about it, and about all he said was 'It's got 14,000 miles on it.' I said, "What about rust?" and he said, 'It's only been rained on a couple of times. You just have to come and see the car.'"

Pardo insists he wasn't looking for a pristine survivor car when he happened upon the Bel Air sedan, but when he began finding things like a date on the original trunk mat, and original dealer stickers in the door jamb (from Allen Chevrolet, in Hagerstown, Ind.), he began to realize what an unblemished specimen the car was.

The 1955s ushered in a whole new era for Chevrolet, and the top-tier Bel Air was Chevy's "little Cadillac."

"In '96 they had it tuned up and of course threw away the wires and spark plug wires, and they had the fuel pump changed," he said. "Why, I don't know, because it only had 14,000 miles on it. But they still had the original one and I got it and had it rebuilt! I don't have it on the car, but I still have the original fuel pump."

"The heater hoses have been changed, too, but all the little spring clamps, all that stuff's original on it. They had a new set of blackwalls put on it. Somebody had told the guy back in 1972 that the tires weren't any good.... But then [the son] says, 'Those original tires are in the barn, do you want 'em?' So I got all the original tires. I cleaned them up and got 'em out of any light. I'm just saving them. I wouldn't put 'em on ... but it looks like they would probably hold air. They've got lots of tread, just maybe a little dry rot. The car had 11,000 miles on it when they took them off."

It's safe to say not many 1955 Bel Airs were so ignored during their earlier years. They were simply some of the most popular vehicles the car buying public had ever seen up that point and their popularity among new car buyers of 1955 is matched today by collectors who have made the '55 Chevys part of the "Tri-Five" trio of hobby royalty.

With its all-new styling and technical features, the '55 Chevy was formidable competition for just about everybody in its day. Its upgraded image pushed model year output to 1,766,013 units, which was more than 300,000 ahead of Ford.

Buyers who wanted to spend $100 to $150 above the mid-tier Two-Ten price could get the dressy-looking Bel Air. Standard equipment on the top-of-the-line models included carpets on closed body styles, a chrome ribbed headliner on the sport coupe, richer upholstery fabrics, horizontal chrome strips on the sides of the front fender and doors, narrow white-painted inserts on the fear fender size moldings, gold Bel Air scripts and Chevrolet crests behind slanting vertical sash moldings, wide chrome window and door post moldings (on sedan models) and full-wheel discs.

The base 235-cid six-cylinder came in 123-hp solid lifter and 136-hp hydraulic lifter versions — the latter was standard with Powerglide, but optional otherwise. The new Turbo-Fire V-8 engine options started with the 265-cid, 162-hp two-barrel. A "Power-Pack" version featured a four-barrel carb and 180 hp.

Pardo's car has the two-barrel V-8 and all the usual Bel Air amenities except one; for some reason, the radio was curiously deleted. "Yeah, it's got no radio," he said. "It's got the cigarette lighter; dual outside mirrors, which were extra; the wide whitewalls, which were extra; electric wipers. It's got about all the options, except the Power-Pack. But to have so much stuff and then no radio?"

His only repair work so far has been cleaning up one of the front brakes that he thought might be hanging up. "It was pulling real hard to the left, so I figured the right one wasn't working," he said. "One of these days I want to clean up the left one, too."

Even after owning the car for more than three years and putting roughly 3,000 miles on it, Pardo is amazed at the car's immaculate condition. "It's just phenomenal," he said. "Really, it's just an unreal car. People call me and come to see it to use the stampings and markings for their restorations. They'll come and measure something, and then leave and go work on their own cars …

"If you look real close, you can see one nick on one of the rocker panels, I think that's where the seat belt hit it. And it's got a dent about half the size of your fist on one corner of the rear bumper. People ask me about that, and I tell them that's the way it's going to stay because that's the way I got it… And if you look in the trunk you can find some very, very small spots of brown. But that's about it."

Ironically, Pardo had plenty of other '55 Chevys when he was young, and they were all on the opposite end of the condition scale. "In Indiana, those cars used to all rust out on the bottom and rot into the ground," he said. "We used to race them a lot at the track. There were no floorboards in them, which is why I liked them. They were light!"

Now, Pardo is looking for someone that wants to be the caretaker for a car that has obviously been meticulously cared for its entire life. He's hoping to find a sedan with similar virtues that is a little more suited to cruising and joy riding.

"Down to the end of the road and back is 8/10 of a mile," he says with a laugh. "I do know that! That's about it for this car."

CHAPTER 13 | **1957 BEL AIR SEDAN**

Story and photos by Angelo Van Bogart

'TWO-FOUR' FOUR-DOOR FAUX PAS

A '57 Bel Air with four doors and eight barrels? Yup, Chevy built at least one

In addition to a healthy amount of dealer-mounted accessories, this never-restored 1957 Chevrolet Bel Air sedan was ordered with two four-barrel carburetors, identified as an "eight barrel" setup on the original build sheet. The car was recently purchased by Larry Fisette of De Pere, Wis. Only full-size Chevrolets with the dual-four-barrel setup were given the famous "bat-wing" air cleaner; Corvettes received individual air cleaner "pots." The Chevrolet's bat-wing design was shared with Cadillacs of the era.

56

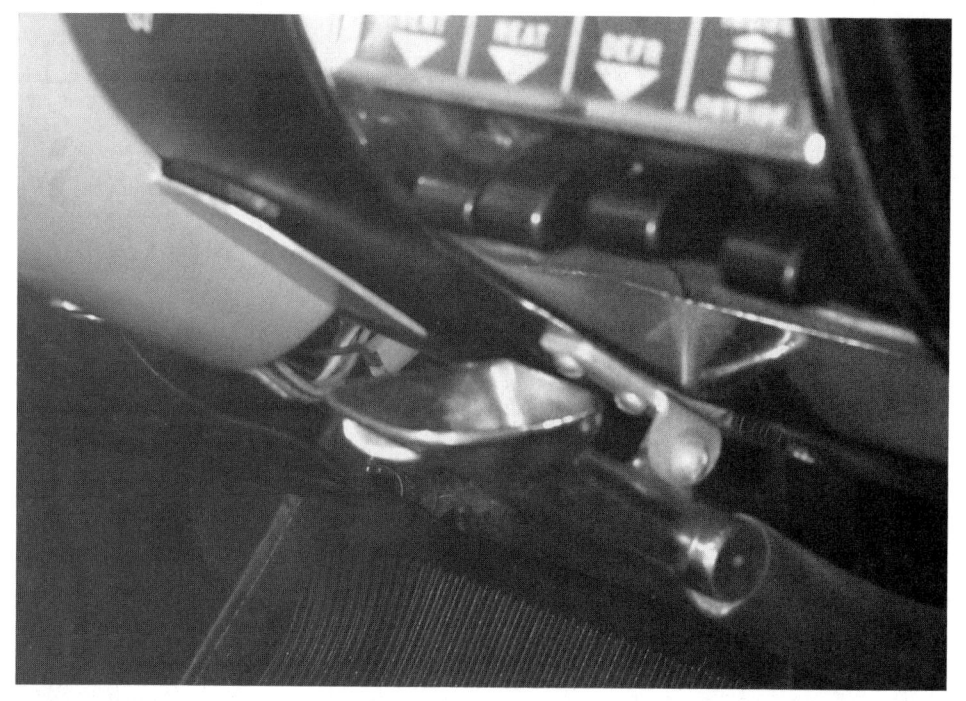

Besides the dual-four-barrel setup, this 1957 Chevrolet is further loaded with accessories, including a smokeless ash tray. The original owner said these accessories were already on the car when he bought it for "around $3,000."

It's a scene that's been played out on streets and strips over and over again, from America's heartland to its coasts:

A '57 Chevy Bel Air crawls up to the line, even with its challenger. Engines rev, the light turns green, tires squeal and the cars charge ahead. When the Chevy gains the upper hand, its competitor first gets a glimpse of the hash marks behind the hooded headlamps, then looks for the fuel injection emblem in front of the door as the Chevy pulls ahead. The challenger looks to his speedometer, then ahead again, but that Bel Air side trim sweeps past him, crossing the door and falling down the rear fender. Soon, all that's visible of the Chevy is its sharp, sinister tailfins and crescent-shaped tail lamps as it claims the win.

But this '57 Chevy story has a twist — a black and lemon yellow twist.

The scene is North Dakota, and the Chevrolet Bel Air is still a winner. But instead of getting a glimpse of one door of the Chevy, the loser racing against this '57 Bel Air gets a view of two doors — on the same side of the car.

How this Colonial Cream and Onyx Black sleeper sedan came to be is probably

Above, A legit dual-quad-equipped, full-size 1957 Chevrolet should have these brackets on the front of the 283's valve covers. Right, The hidden gas cap is even an accessory locking unit, made thin enough to fit in the tailfin of the '57 Chevy.

nothing more than a mistake, and while most such mistakes are overlooked, overcome or erased and then forgotten, this error has come to be cherished and preserved.

Lake Chevrolet in Devils Lake, N.D., is responsible for the fortunate faux pas that resulted in a family-friendly 1957 Chevrolet Bel Air four-door sedan equipped with the race-worthy 245-hp, dual-quad 283-cid V-8 — an engine powerful enough to back up Chevy's "Hot One" catch phrase.

"[Dealership co-owner] Gene Bergstrom made a mistake… he must have pushed too many buttons when he ordered it," said Earl Besse, the original owner of the two-four-barrel-equipped 1957 Chevrolet Bel Air sedan shown here.

"I did most of the ordering of the cars, but I don't remember [ordering] that one, but it's quite possible" added Bergstrom, who clearly remembers Besse and his yellow '57 Chevy. "We'd order something different once in a while."

Regardless of how this '57 came to be, it doesn't take an experienced salesman to know that a hot, dual-carbureted engine

In case a wheel cover flew off, the original owner wrote his name on the back of each so it could be returned. Each signature is still present.

in a bread-and-butter sedan in the middle of farm country would be a tough sell in 1957. No fuel consumption-conscious farm wife would have wanted a petrol-slamming eight-barrel Chevy to carry the kids to baseball practice or to pick up ingredients for apple pie at the local market. And no gearhead graduate would have wanted a 245-hp small-block V-8 in a sedan that would have looked right at home in the parking lot of the local Methodist church.

Larry Fisette, the current owner of this special Chevrolet, worked at Curran Chevrolet in Manistique, Mich., in 1957, and he knows the makeup of the average Chevrolet bought and sold at that time. As such, he knows this isn't a typical 1957 Chevrolet.

"You'd see the six-cylinder sticks all day, and you'd get excited about a V-8 Power Pack," Fisette said of his days at the dealership. Nodding at his recently purchased dual-quad '57 Bel Air sedan, he added, "You wouldn't have been able to give that car to anybody."

The 90-year-old Besse doesn't recall why he walked into Lake Chevrolet on June 13, 1957, but he does know why he raced that dual-quad sedan home.

"I don't know why I was looking, to tell you the truth, but I always like a new car, a new tractor," Besse said. "I told my wife I was going to Devils Lake, and she and my youngest boy got in the car."

They drove to Lake Chevrolet and found the yellow-and-black Bel Air in the dealership's basement. Either the color or the engine caught Besse's attention, and he told the salesman, "Let's go for a ride."

"I took it for a ride and was going 70, gave it gas and we were going 120," Besse said. "I turned back around and bought it."

For a father with a bit of a lead foot, like Besse, the fast four-door had the perfect combination. Sure, he got in trouble with the highway patrol every now and again for speeding, but it also made a great family car for driving around Devils Lake or vacationing to California. The Bel Air may look sedate, but Besse is quick to point out the

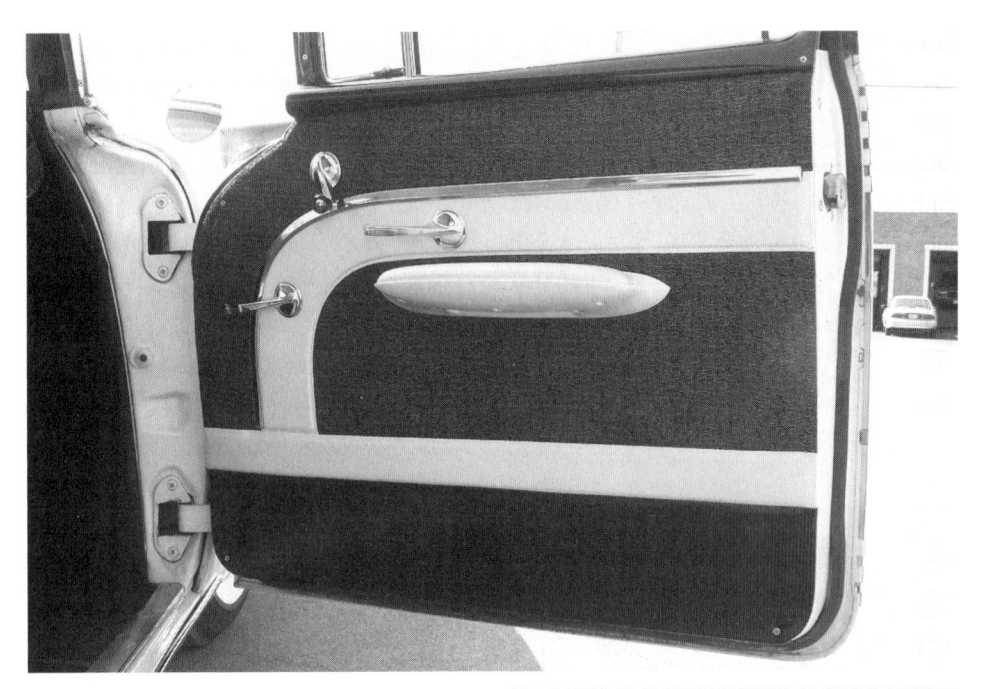

This unrestored Bel Air sedan has a combination of cloth, vinyl and a rubberized material on the seats in yellow and black to match the exterior.

sedan's "dark side."

"It is dangerous...it will go 125 mph — that's a lot!" Besse said. "I was in good with the highway patrol back then. They'd pull me over and ask, 'Is that you Earl?'

"I didn't mind driving it fast and it didn't mind going fast — that car would never get hurt. It was hard on tires and mufflers, though, so we put on special mufflers, but you'd never have to touch that motor. It'll go 150,000 miles, I think. It didn't matter how fast or slow you go, it doesn't burn a drop of oil."

The stealthy Bel Air's prowess also saved

the car from an uncertain future when Besse was finally ready to part with it in the late 1980s. The second owner of the car nearly bought it for someone who probably wasn't ready to be a steward of such a rare car in fine, original condition.

"When I sold it to some guy, he was going to give it to his kid for a graduation present, but after he bought it, he decided it was too hot for his son," Besse recalled.

Fortunately, the Chevrolet was spared the potential horrors in the hands of some four-door-loathing youth, whose inexperience could have resulted in new paint over the original Colonial Cream and Onyx Black, or bucket seats in place of the original black, yellow and silver bench seat or, worse yet, the removal of its highly desirable two-four-barrel setup for use in a more desirable two-door. Its original documentation — which includes the build sheet denoting the "411N 8 bbl carb," the new car inspection and adjustment form, owner service policy and more — could have been misplaced in college textbooks or disposed of altogether. Instead, the car remained with seasoned hobbyists who recognized its uniqueness and fine original condition.

Since Besse sold the car in the late 1980s with around 55,000 miles, its relatively short list of subsequent owners have used it conservatively, keeping the miles down and the car in unrestored condition. When current owner Fisette first stumbled upon it in late 2009, the car was showing its current 65,000 spins of the odometer. But he didn't seal the deal until February of this year.

A friend of Fisette found the car in an online auction around Christmas time, but bidding didn't reach the reserve. Fisette then contacted the seller.

"I told him I was buying the car, but it was up to him when, because we were several thousand dollars apart," Fisette said. "We stayed in contact for several months, and after we agreed on a price, it was in my garage 24 hours later."

Fisette has owned hundreds of cars in his lifetime, including his fair share of "Tri-Chevys," and is probably most famous for finding the 21 trailers full of muscle cars, Corvettes and parts in Wisconsin, but this '57 Chevrolet is particularly special to him. It's a connection that also runs deeper than his employment at Chevrolet dealerships in the late 1950s.

"I have not had a car that is as exciting to me as that car, and I think I've owned about every damn thing you can," Fisette said. "That car turns me on, the combo… It's the car that shouldn't have been.

"If my dad had gone to a dealership in 1957, he wouldn't have bought that car under any circumstance. But it would have been nice if it was my dad's car."

Most dads would have opted for the Blue Flame six-cylinder, or perhaps the Turbo-Fire 265-cid V-8. The two-barrel 283-cid Super Turbo-Fire V-8 landed in a good many 1957 Chevrolets, while the "Power Pack" four-barrel, dual-exhaust 283-cid V-8 also wound up in a fair amount of 1957 Chevys, especially exciting two-door hardtops and convertibles.

1957 marked the first year Chevrolet became serious about going fast. As if the dizzying number of V-8s already mentioned didn't offer enough choice, Chevrolet had a group of four particularly potent V-8 performance engines available for the 1957 model year.

The 245-hp, 283-cid V-8 with two four barrels and hydraulic lifters — as in Fisette's 1957 Chevrolet — represented the first rung in the ladder of performance Chevrolets that year. A second dual-four-barrel 283-cid engine with solid lifters provided 270 hp, or by ordering the exotic new fuel injection system on the 283-cid V-8, 250 hp with hydraulic lifters or 283 hp with solid lifters and a Duntov cam was available. These potent engines were often found in lowly One-Fifty two-door sedans for racing use, highly optioned Bel Air two-door models, and the occasional Two-Ten Sport Coupe and two-door sedan. But almost never in any series of Chevrolet with more than two doors.

Since many 1957 Chevrolets are fitted with fuel injection or dual four-barrel-carburetor systems during the restoration process to increase their value, Fisette was skeptical of whether this four-door 1957 Chevrolet was built by the factory as a 245-hp car. Thanks to the car's original condition and its matching patina throughout, plus mountains of original paperwork, Fisette was convinced that this car was the real deal.

"I was skeptical, but all the documents proved it," Fisette said. "It's got no issues if it has the tissues."

After Fisette got the car home, the Bel Air sedan whispered the rest of its story. Original tags hung from their correct location on the carburetors and rear end, the original hardware for the dual-four setup was in place, and the correct deep-groove pulleys on the water pump, generator and harmonic balancer were as they should be. The Bel Air also had its original dual-quad valve covers, though they were scratched and chipped, and each retained its special mount to support the "pots" of the batwing-shaped oil bath air cleaner.

While flipping through the car's paperwork, Fisette noticed service records showing the Bel Air was maintained by Lake Chevrolet through the late 1980s, and that one of the registration cards from that time period had a handwritten phone number on the front. On the off-chance the number might still be good, Fisette called it. On the other end of the phone was original owner Earl Besse, who verified the car's as-built configuration.

A local DePere, Wis., 1957 Chevrolet expert also stopped by to study the car and was excited to see such an intact and original '57 with dual-quads. He admitted that he had never seen a build sheet for a 1957 Chevrolet, as it's quite a rarity today.

The original paint retains the original dealership sticker, and both the original owner and Lake Chevrolet are still going strong in Devils Lake, N.D.

"The expert said it still has the correct fuel pump, water pump, heads, radiator, carburetors...," Fisette said, adding that the car retains the factory tool kit in the trunk. He admitted that he wasn't aware '57 Chevys had such an accessory, and he's not only owned many Tri-Chevys in the past 50 years, he worked around them since the cars were new.

While the car is a nice original, it's by no means perfect. The black paint on the batwing air cleaner is chipped, the Colonial Cream paint on the body shows signs of use and the chrome has lost some luster. Normally, Fisette would consider detailing or partially restoring a car such as this one by addressing its most obvious faults, but he's leaving this sedan as he found it.

"I was going to lift the body off the frame and detail the engine and chassis," he said.

"I think it's remarkable that the car even has its original air cleaner — I considered repainting it, but I can't bring myself to do it."

Instead, Fisette left the perfect-idling carburetors and whisper-quiet engine alone, merely tuning up the powerplant by installing NOS spark plugs and points in the dual-point distributor and serviced the brakes. And when the Wisconsin roads are clear of winter salt, he'll drive it, at least until it finds its next owner and Fisette stumbles onto his next "find."

"I really like the car, but I just have to find the guy who likes it better," Fisette said. "For me, it's all about the chase."

Although its home may be temporary, something tells us this Bel Air understands the chase, having had a few of its own back in the day.

CHAPTER 14 — 1958 CHEVROLET LINEUP
By Phil Hall

ONE-YEAR WONDERS: THE 1958 CHEVYS

For 1958, the new Delray series replaced the old One-Fifty lineup. Although it was at the bottom of the Chevrolet ladder, this Delray two-door sedan sports wide whitewall tires and full wheel covers.

The words "all-new" are often overused in automotive circles, most often incorrectly referring to warmed-over "new" models. Fifty years ago, "all-new" really meant something when attached to the just-introduced 1958 Chevrolet passenger cars.

They had all-new body, chassis, rear suspension and steering designs. Model lineups were redone, and there even was a new V-8 engine thrown in for good measure.

While the 1957 Chevrolets today are considered all-time classics, back in 1957, they were on the third year of a styling cycle and had to compete with all-new 1957 Fords and Plymouths. Ford scored a rare victory in model-year sales, and something had to be done.

While its two main competitors were

The star of the 1958 Chevrolet lineup was the Bel Air Impala convertible, the perfect car to take to a private picnic. This example is decked out with a continental kit and fender skirts.

warmed over for 1958, Chevrolet brought a near totally redone lineup of passenger cars.

Bodies were completely restyled and were mounted on a new "Safety-Girder" frame, which featured X-type construction with three cross members and a center tube. Rear suspension design changed from traditional leaf springing to coils with three control arms. Up front, there was new steering with a jointed steering shaft and steering pieces ahead of the front wheels.

New bodies and underpinnings all resulted in a longer, lower and wider package that, on the average, was 150 pounds heavier. Wheelbase grew from 115 to 117.5 inches; overall length grew from around 200 to 209.1 inches. Width ballooned from 73.7 to 77.5 inches. Height dropped, depending on the model, nearly 4 inches to just over 56. The X-frame permitted the reduced height without loss of passenger room. Quad headlamps were standard for the first time on a Chevrolet production car.

The mid-level Chevrolet for '58 was the Biscayne series. The line included only four-door sedans and two-door sedans, like the two-tone example here.

A new lineup added to the excitement. Stars of the show were the Bel Air Impala two-door hardtop and convertible. Hardtops featured styling cues from the 1956 Chevrolet Motorama Impala dream car with reverse-angle rear window pillars and a simulated rear roof vent. There were also simulated vents on the rear quarter panels, six tail lamps, an interior with three-tone seat inserts, reflectors in the extended armrests and, in hardtops, a pull-up center armrest in the middle of the back seat, among other standout features.

However, Impalas were only part of the Bel Air stable. There also was a more conventional Sport Coupe (two-door hardtop), Sport Sedan (four-door hardtop) plus two- and four-door sedans.

Replacing the Two-Ten mid-range series was the Biscayne, taking a name from the 1955 Chevy dream car, a four-door hardtop. However, there were no hardtop Biscaynes this time around, ending a Chevy mid-range tradition. Only two- and four-door sedans were offered.

Holding down the bottom rung replac-

The Bel Air Sport Sedan four-door hardtop was a fine-looking car with plenty of top-of-the-line bright trim. Only the Bel Air line offered a pillarless four-door.

ing the One-Fifty was the Delray series, its name coming from a fancy version of Two-Ten two-door sedans of past years. Two- and four-door sedans resided here, plus a business coupe.

Station wagons were given their own series for 1958, not carrying the same series designations of the other models as in the past. At the top was the Nomad, but stylish two-doors of the past were just a memory. A pillared four-door, six passenger wagon now carried the name that began on a 1954 Corvette-styled dream car. Nomads were equal to Bel Airs in trim level.

Patterned after Biscaynes were Brookwoods, in four-door six- and nine-passenger versions. Yeoman carried the new designation for the lower-priced wagons. Two- and four-door models were offered, all carrying six passengers.

One of the few areas where major carryover components were used was in the engine compartment.

Back again was the traditional Blue-Flame 235.5-cid six and 283 Turbo-Fire V-8. However, a third design joined the lineup, the Turbo-Thrust 348-cid V-8. More on that in a minute.

A compression ratio kicked the Blue Flame's horsepower up five to 145. The original small-block 265 V-8 was gone for 1958 and replaced as the standard V-8 by the 185-horsepower Turbo-Fire with 8.5:1 compression and a two-barrel carburetor.

Next up came the Super Turbo-Fire 283 with a four-barrel and 9.5:1 compression, with a rating of 230 hp. Ramjet Fuel Injection came next at 250 hp and 9.5:1. Though not heavily advertised, you could obtain the Corvette fuel-injection unit at 290 horses, hot cam, solid lifters and 10.5 squeeze.

It was common knowledge that bigger cubes would be needed for 1958, as Ford would have a new 352 and Plymouth 350 with bigger blocks.

Expanding the 283 to that size would be years away, so Chevy drew on a truck engine it had under design, the W-engine. At 348 cubic inches, it was right in the ballpark. Slightly larger than the 283, it weighed about 100 pounds more. Among its features were combustion chambers in the block and inverted W-shaped heads. The Turbo-Thrust was rather mild with hydraulic lifters, mild cam and 9.5:1 compression. With a single four-barrel carb, rating came in at 250 horsepower. Triple two-barrel Rochesters boosted the advertised rating to 280.

Domestic automobile manufacturers agreed to stop participating in racing and cut back on new performance engines, and Chevrolet division followed most of the edict. However, under the guise of law enforcement development, a mid-year 348 option was released, with solid lifters, 11:1 compression, triple two-barrels and 315 advertised horsepower.

With no factory backing, most Chevrolet stock car racers chose to stick with the 1957 models, the 1958s being too big and two different. There were some 1958 models raced that season, however.

With a purpose of retaking the industry sales lead, 1958 Chevrolets sold less than their less-than-popular 1957 counterparts, but wait, there's more. It turned out that 1958 was a recession year, and though Chevrolet model-year production dropped from just over 1.5 million to north of 1.2 million, Ford dived to less than a million, giving Chevrolet the crown... big time.

As it turned out, 1958 Chevrolets were one-year wonders. Reacting to the radical 1957 Chrysler Corp. styling, GM went all-new across the board for the 1959 model year — at least as bodies went.

It took a while for the automotive world to appreciate the 1958 Chevrolets, as among collectors and racers, they lived in the shadow of the 1955-'57 models for many years. However, customizers warmed to the first Impalas right from the start. Restorers and collectors eventually followed.

Even young Chevy enthusiasts were attracted to the 1958 models early, as that was the year the popular 3-in-1 AMT/SMP 1:25 plastic customizing kits hit the market, using the basic promo dies with custom and racing parts and decals in the kit. Both the Impala convertible and hardtop models were offered. Since then, 1958 Chevy Impalas have been a staple of the model car hobby.

CHAPTER 15 | **1959 IMPALA CONVERTIBLE**

Story and photos by John Gunnell

CAT'S MEOW
Gloria J. Mihna and her '59-er' from Medina

Gloria Minah enjoys driving her '59 ragtop with "cat's eye" tail lamps while wearing 1950s-style "cat's-eye" sunglasses. She drove the car to high school and says she used half of every paycheck to fix the car.

"I'm Gloria J. Mihna, I live in Medina and I have a 1959 Chevy convertible, white with a turquoise interior," said the proud owner of a drop-top Impala that will probably never leave the village of Medina, Wis. "It's my first car. I've had it since June of 1971.

"It was my only car, winter and summer, for years, and I have turned down an offer of $100,000 for it."

Gloria's purchase of the car was a family affair of sorts. Gloria's father liked 1960 Chevrolets and owned 13 of them at one time. The 1959 Chevy was also the first car that her brother, Gary Hansen, owned. He purchased it for $400 in the summer of 1967 in Turlock, Calif., while living in Modesto.

"I drove the car for two years until the transmission went out," Gary said. "After it broke, I didn't have money to fix it and my boss sold me a '65 GTO on payments." When Gary's Impala-loving dad came out to the West Coast to move Gary home, he made Gary sell it to him for $1, put a transmission in it and drove it back to Waupaca, Wis., where the family lived then.

When she turned 16, Gloria Hansen took her driver's license test in her father's 1960 Impala convertible. Then she drove the 1959 convertible to high school. The original plan was that Gloria's father would give her the car as a graduation present, and she used half of each paycheck she earned at the time to buy things for the car, such as a $150 convertible top.

Other money went towards buying pots and pans, because Chris Minha and Gloria wanted to get married.

"Dad sat Chris and I down and said, 'If you get married that car comes back to me,'" Gloria recalled. "He said, 'If you can buy cookware you can buy the car,' so I went to the bank and got $350 out and he signed the car totally over to me. Twenty years later, I told my mom I never got my graduation present. She had no idea I had bought the car, and she sent me a graduation card and $20."

When Chris and Gloria got married in

1974, the convertible was their wedding car.

"Today, we use it for other peoples' weddings," Gloria laughed. She drove the car in the summer when it was 90 degrees and in winter when it was 20 below. "I would tuck a blanket down inside the back seat and back window so I could use it in winter," Gloria remembered. "Once, the speedometer cable got so cold it made a cranking noise and went 'ping,' and after that, I had no way of knowing how fast I was going, but I knew I was going fast!"

With its 348-cid V-8, the car was always a mover, and today both the engine number and Powerglide transmission number remain matching units, and both have been rebuilt. The Impala also has power brakes, dual exhaust and Gloria still has the original radio, although a Custom Autosound replacement is mounted in the dash opening. The clock and the steering wheel are original, but the yellow-and-blue Playboy Bunny stickers on the dash are something that Gloria added in her high school days.

"I told Chris I will never remove those bunnies," she said. "All my other memories have been taken off the car, but the bunnies are staying."

At one point, the car got so rusty that a skinny little friend of Gloria's put her foot down on the floorboard and it went right through to the blacktop. Gloria had the car repaired several times while it was in regular use. Then, in 1980, the electrical wiring went out and it sat in the garage for the next 20 years. In 2000, Gloria decided to have the car restored. Expert body man John McHugh — locally known as "Magoo" — spent 3-1/2 months making the Chevy's body look new again and Erickson Upholstery redid the interior.

"The car had a lot of body work done and we got a lot of parts from CARS, I think," said Gloria. "Fond du Lac Bumper Exchange re-chromed the original bumpers, including the one-piece California rear bumper. Automotive Specialists in Neenah, Wis., redid the original engine and transmission." Gloria had to get a new deck lid, because the old one became very rusty just from sitting in her garage. All the other rust-damaged body panels were repaired and repainted by Magoo.

After the car was restored, Gloria started taking it to shows, and she now goes to about 10 events per year.

"The License to Cruise in downtown Appleton was the first place I ever showed it," Gloria recalled. "The photographer for the show stopped me and took a picture of the back of the car and they put me in a premium spot so everyone could see the gull-wing rear end." Gloria always drives the Chevy to shows and never trailers it. The car is her pride and joy.

"It was my first car and it will stay with me until I die; I will never sell it," says Gloria. "Until I'm in a body bag, this car stays with me. My husband can get the car after I'm gone, but I could never imagine anyone else driving my car but Chris and me. It won't happen. It's my true love for a car — I had it before I had my husband."

CHAPTER 16 | **1960 CHEVY IMPALA**

Story and photos by John Gunnell

NOMADIC IMPALA
Unrestored '60 criss-crossed country for 50 years before landing home

Only 22,081 original miles show on this survivor car's speedometer. The Chevrolet crest and "V" in the central grille insert indicate a V-8 engine behind the grille.

The stunning 1960 Chevrolet Impala convertible featured here was a true three-owner survivor car, at least until Stefano Bimbi bought it at a Dana Mecum auction in Monterey, Calif. Bimbi — the owner of Nickey Chicago in St. Charles, Ill. — was amazed at the car's originality and state of condition. Strangely enough, in passing through his hands, the car wound up going "home."

In researching the vehicle, Bimbi found that the Impala's first owners were originally from Indiana. Afterwards, they moved to Colorado. While in their possession, the Impala was always garaged and very well cared for. After a few years, they sold it to the second owner, who cared for it until 1981.

The car's odometer showed 22,000 miles in 1981, the year it was sold to a third person on the East Coast. The day the car was delivered, he parked it in his garage and never drove it again. He was afraid to damage or de-value the car, so it sat until after he died. At that point, his widow contacted Wayne Carini of Chasing Classic Cars and asked for helping selling the car.

Carini and his crew cleaned the car up and brought it to the Mecum Auction in Monterey. The car was featured in one of Mecum's televised auction segments. The film crew turned their cameras on Bimbi while he was inspecting the car, which he then purchased.

Mecum modestly described the car as: "All original; 22,000 miles, believed to be actual from new; never restored; purchased in 1981 by third owner; stored in garage and not moved until June of 2009; power steering; power brakes; automatic transmission." After Bimbi brought the car home and looked it over very closely, he realized that it was truly an exceptional automobile.

"It even had its original top and five original tires," Stefano notes. "I had never seen a floor covering made of vinyl that wasn't cracked or missing chunks and pieces. It was the most showroom-original 1960 Chevy I had ever seen!"

Due to the car's amazing originality and quality, Bimbi had noted Chevrolet memorabilia expert Tom Dietz clean it up. Dietz is an experienced Impala collector and restorer and he took the car to the next level with his super detailing. The car was then

The red-and-white seats were the fashion rage of 1960 and give the car a nostalgic appearance today.

sold to a private museum. Believe it or not, it wound up going back to Indiana, the same state in which it was originally owned.

In 1960, this Impala model was the only full-size ragtop that Chevrolet offered. The big convertible featured a modernized version of the gull-wing rear end styling introduced a year earlier. Small, circular tail lamps that appeared on the first Impala of 1958 and then became a Chevy trademark for more than another decade replaced the cat's-eye tail lamps of 1959. The convertible was offered in a six-cylinder version with a starting price of $2,921 or a small-block V-8 version that retailed for $3,028 and up.

Both cars shared a 119-inch wheelbase and measured 210.8 inches end to end. The curb weight was 3,625 lbs. for the six and the base V-8 was only 10 more pounds. The base 235-cid 135-hp inline engine was Chevrolet's famous "Stovebolt Six." The standard V-8 was a 283-cid 170-hp job named Super Turbo-Fire. Chevrolet built 8,839 six-cylinder convertibles versus 71,065 V-8 convertibles. Today, both cars — in excellent condition — are easily worth more than 10 times what they sold for when new.

CHAPTER 17 | 1960 CORVAIR

By Phil Hall

A WELCOME STRANGER
Sporty flair helped early Corvair sales

The Corvair Monza 900 club coupe was introduced mid-year 1960. The model became the most expensive car in the Corvair line that year.

At first glance, the mid-year 1960 Chevrolet Corvair five-passenger club coupe didn't look right. The greenhouse was too small, and the Corvair wasn't all that big to begin with.

As it turned out, the compact coupe turned out to be just what was needed to make the rear-engine, air-cooled, six-cylinder-powered car a success.

In the fall of 1959, the long-awaited compact cars from the domestic "Big Three" manufacturers came to market. Ford's Falcon was the least controversial with pleasant styling and a conventional drivetrain. Chrysler Corp.'s Valiant also had a conventional drivetrain (if you call

The Corvair convertible appeared only in the Monza line in 1963. Just over 44,000 of the drop-tops left the dealerships. This number included the 7,472 equipped with the Spyder package.

the slant-six conventional), but more offbeat styling. Corvair's rear engine was more closely related to the German Volkswagen than the full-sized Chevrolet.

Falcon turned out to be the runaway best seller of the trio. Corvair wound up second, but needed some help.

Initially, the Corvair came only in four-door-sedan form, in 700 and base (later called 500) series. Stories of cooling fan belt troubles on the early cars put a damper on demand.

The five-passenger club coupe came along in January, offered in both the 700 and 500 series. It was an answer to the Falcon two-doors. It would take until the 1961 model year for Valiant to get its two-door models.

Dressed-up show cars were common at the time, and a specially equipped Corvair coupe appeared at the Chicago Auto Show in February. Featuring bucket-type front seats, chromed door and window frames, fancy wheels, trick paint and a sunroof, the Monza show car caught the show goers' attention. Its popularity led to a production version, labeled the Monza 900. It appeared in showrooms in spring, minus the sunroof.

The Corvair 700 club coupe for 1961 was the mid-level two-door in the Corvair line-up, sitting between the lower-priced 500 club coupe and the high-priced Monza club coupe. The 700 club coupe featured a bright belt moulding around the body.

It should be noted that sales literature referred to the car as just plain "Monza," but fender badges said Monza 900. This contrast continued into the 1963 model year.

With chrome-trimmed front buckets, a floor shift when equipped with the standard three-speed manual transmission, and a list price of $2,238 (nearly $200 more than the 700), Chevrolet had a sports compact with no domestic competition. Despite the late start, nearly 12,000 Monza 900s were sold.

Though other domestic cars had bucket-type front seats at the time, Monza popularized the idea in the compact class and would launch a fleet of "bucket brigade" imitators in the months ahead.

For 1961, Corvairs had minor changes. Not satisfied with just a coupe, a Monza 900 four-door sedan was added. A front bench seat was standard with buckets optional. Four-speed manual transmissions were now optional for Corvairs, adding to the Monza's sporting credentials.

New-car buyers bought the Monza 900 concept with 109,945 coupes being sold, making it the most popular Corvair model. Monza four-doors went out the showroom doors 33,745 times.

Before the club coupe came along, the Corvair four-door sedan was the only body style produced in 1960. The model shown here is a DeLuxe 700. The car was popular, with 139,208 examples sold.

Things got even better for 1962 when an all-time record of 151,738 Monza 900 coupes were sold. The coupe had plenty of company in the series, as a short-lived Monza four-door wagon was announced. Mid-season, the Monza convertible came along, a far more sporting offering. Rag-top sales came in at 16,569 cars.

Also mid-year 1962, a Spyder option was offered for the Monza coupe and convertible. Among the features were a turbocharged engine rated at 150 horsepower and special instrumentation. Though few were ordered in Spyder trim (2,569 coupes and 2,779 convertibles), they would go on to become some of the most desirable Corvairs of all time.

Meanwhile, bread-and-butter Corvair 500 and 700 sales were slowing down, thanks to the introduction of the Chevy II conventional compact lineup for 1962.

Corvairs continued basically the same for 1963 and 1964, but sales continued to slide. The Monza 900 coupe produced

A specially prepared Corvair club coupe appeared at the Chicago Auto Show in the early 1960s. The car featured bucket seats, chromed door and window frames, fancy wheels, trick paint and a sunroof.

129,544 sales (11,627 Spyder options) for 1963. For 1964, Monza Spyder became its own series. The 900 badge was gone from the fenders that year. Monza coupe sales dropped to 88,440 for 1964, and Spyders generated 6,480 customers.

Perhaps a reason for the accelerated slide in the last two years (especially 1964), was the growing popularity of V-8-powered compacts, which offered greater performance.

No doubt the 1965 Mustang, introduced in April 1964, helped grease the skids.

Corvair got its only complete restyling for 1965, with two- and four-door sedans being replaced by pillarless hardtops. Convertibles continued. Performance improved, but other problems, all too well known, would hurt. The last Corvair was a 1969 model.

CHAPTER 18 | *1961 CORVAIR GREENBRIER*

By Byron Olsen

THE ORIGINAL MINIVAN
Versatile and unique Greenbrier was a Corvair at heart

The 1961 Chevrolet Corvair Greenbrier was the "big three's" first minivan built with small-car components and with car-like features, and its success was short-lived. By the time this 1965 Corvair Greenbrier minivan was offered, sales for the vehicle were deeply waning. (Byron Olsen collection)

It is generally recognized that the minivan revolution in the U.S. began with the 1984 introduction of the Dodge Caravan and Plymouth Voyager. In contrast with other passenger vans then available from American manufacturers, which were based on truck chassis, the new Caravan and Voyager were smaller and drove more like cars than trucks. There was a good reason for that: the drivetrain, chassis components, and platform were derived from the Chrysler "K" cars. It wasn't long before the

Not only could a Corvair Greenbrier owner select optional left side doors to provide access to the rear seats, but the windows in these rear doors could be rolled down. Even when the left side doors were not ordered, the windows could still be rolled down for rear passenger comfort. (Byron Olsen collection)

Chrysler Corp. minivans virtually replaced the station wagon as America's family car and spawned a raft of imitators. One of the keys to the success of the Chrysler minivans (and something the competition was slow to figure out) was that the Mopar minivans drove like a car instead of a clumsy, downsized truck.

Well, gang, I'm here to tell you that the Caravan/Voyager were not the first U.S. minivans to be built with car components, easy-to-maneuver small car size, car economy and car handling. That honor belongs to the now-forgotten Chevrolet Corvair Greenbrier, a compact, rear-engine, rear-drive minivan introduced in 1961 as part of the new Corvair compact car line.

The year before, 1960, was the year that Detroit's "big three" finally took notice of America's growing interest in smaller, more economical cars and introduced the compact Ford Falcon, Plymouth Valiant and Chevrolet Corvair. Sales of the German Volkswagen and the U.S. Rambler had been booming, and Detroit was forced to concede that many car buyers had decided that bigger was not necessarily better.

The VW used a rear-mounted, air-cooled engine. That layout became the role model for Chevy's new Corvair. The Corvair was considerably larger than the Volkswagen and used a flat-opposed, six-cylinder engine of a 144 cid instead of the tiny 72-cid four-cylinder in the VW. Horsepower was 80 units in the Corvair compared to a modest 36 bhp in the Volkswagen. But the engines in both cars were air cooled, and both had independent suspension on all four wheels, something unheard of in any other American production car at the time. The Corvair drew much more from European engineering than did its two competitors, the Valiant and the plain-and-simple Falcon.

In the second year of compact car production, each of the "big three" introduced compact-sized passenger and cargo vans to go with their new compact cars. Until this time, small vans set up to carry people had not been built in the U.S. Volkswagen's compact "Microbus," which could seat as many as eight or nine and yet ran with the economy of a VW "Beetle," because it was powered by a Beetle engine, inspired the new crop of American small vans. Ford and Dodge built theirs on downsized truck chassis with solid axles front and rear. They were crude and had their engines stuffed between the two front seats where they took up valuable passenger and cargo room. These vans soon forgot the original concept of compactness and grew into the present huge Dodge Ram and Ford Econoline truck-based vans.

But Chevy again followed the Volkswagen model, this time the Microbus rear-engine, rear-drive box on wheels. The Corvair Greenbrier was the result. By placing the engine and transaxle between and behind the rear wheels, the passenger and cargo area floor could be dropped to the bottom of the vehicle. With no driveshaft or transmission to take up space, this cargo area was unobstructed and at the same time permitted a roof much lower than the competition. With no engine up front, the front seat area was similarly unobstructed and had comfortable seating for three. The drawback was vulnerability to front-end collision crushing.

The finished Greenbrier package was sleek, low and very much in the GM style idiom of the time. Wheelbase was a short 95 inches, less than any contemporary car. Length was a modest 180 inches, the same as the compact Corvair sedans and coupes. Yet, this space contained 175 cubic feet of space, with room for seating as many as nine people. The distance from the back of the front seat to the rear tailgate doors was almost 100 inches. Interior height in the center was 54 inches (40 inches in the rear over the engine compartment).

There was Corvair independent suspension on all four wheels, giving a smooth, supple, compliant ride with decent handling. Weight was a tad under 3,000 pounds. With no engine weight on the front wheels, steering was very easy without any power assistance.

Double side doors gave easy access to the rear seats, and matching double doors could be ordered on the left side as an option. (It took the new generation of minivans a decade to make left side doors available.) There were roll-down windows in every side door, and on the left side, even when doors there were not ordered. Camping equipment and gasoline heaters were among the options.

Mechanically, the Greenbrier used the 144-cid Corvair 80-bhp six-cylinder engine. In 1964, displacement was increased to 164 cid producing 95 bhp with 110 bhp optional. Buyers could choose a three-speed or four-speed manual gearbox, or the Powerglide two-speed automatic. While acceleration was not neck snapping, it was vastly superior to the benchmark VW Microbus, and the Greenbrier could keep up with freeway speeds, something the VW could not.

With all of this room and flexibility and easy car-like handling, the Corvair Greenbrier was an appealing package. Yet, perhaps it was ahead of its time. The Corvair rear-engine, rear-drive concept soon diminished in popularity, and GM quickly turned to conventionally arranged replacements: the Chevy II/Nova car, and front-engine, truck-suspension vans similar to the Ford and Dodge. Greenbrier sales started off at about 18,000 units in 1961 and 1962, but then trailed off to 13,761 in 1963, 6,201 in 1964, and a paltry 1,528 units in 1965, the last year of production.

Chevrolet had clearly lost its enthusiasm for the car by that time, and the lack of advertising push showed it. Yet, the Greenbrier deserved a better fate than that. It was truly the forerunner of the new generation of minivans that would arrive on the scene 20 years later, claiming to be the latest innovation in motoring. Yet we know better: the Greenbrier was there first.

CHAPTER 19 — 1962 CHEVY II
Story by Tom Collins

MASS APPEAL
Chevy II answered demand for economy, performance

Care-free living was even more care-free with the fuel-efficient Chevy II. These beach dwellers are posed with the new-for-1962 Chevrolet Chevy II Nova 400 convertible equipped with a six-cylinder engine.

In 1962, a new car premiered in the Chevrolet lineup. It was born of intense competition created by the success of the 1960 Ford Falcon and Chevrolet's desire to offer a matching conventional vehicle.

Ford, Chrysler Corp. and General Motors each recognized the exploding demand for small cars in the late 1950s. They saw the increasing number of imports from Europe, as well as the success of the Rambler American and the resurgence of Studebaker Corp. with its Lark.

Each of the "Big Three" quickly responded, but only GM went outside the box to introduce the rear-engined, European-influenced Chevrolet Corvair, followed by the front-engine and rear transaxle setup of the Pontiac Tempest. But there was nothing

1962 Economy Car Sales

Falcon	Chevy II	Corvair	Rambler American	Valiant	Lancer
Ford	Chevrolet	Chevrolet	American Motors	Plymouth	Dodge
474,191	326,607	292,531	98,432	97,914	64,271

Source: "Standard Catalog of American Cars 1946-1975"

like the Corvair on this side of the Atlantic Ocean, and that was both the car's strengths and weaknesses.

During the 1960 model year, the Ford Falcon became the sales winner while the Valiant from Chrysler Corp. also had a strong showing. The Corvair had a different appeal with its ultra-modern looks. It was also a pricey choice for buyers.

The simple Falcon sold 435,676 copies, compared to the Corvair with 250,007 editions. Those figures immediately caught the attention of GM executives like nothing since the premier of the Virgil Exner-influenced "Suddenly It's 1960" 1957 finned wonders from Chrysler Corp.

GM wasn't about to yield an automotive niche to anyone without a struggle. It decided it was time for Chevrolet to offer more. The choice was made to take on Falcon directly — dimension for dimension. The new Chevrolet earned the James Bond-like code name H-35 while in development. The timeline was just 18 months to get it ready for 1962 model introductions late in 1961.

The compact Ford Falcon had a 109.5-inch wheelbase and was 181.2 inches long. For its H-35 project, Chevrolet added one-half inch in the wheelbase and just more than a half-inch overall. The project car soon gained the name Chevy II.

The Chevy II was just 200 lbs. heavier than the Falcon when it was equipped with its four-cylinder engine and weighed 342 lbs. more than the Falcon with the six-cylinder engine. The Falcon fell into a price range of $1,985 to just more than $2,600. The base Chevy II 100 two-door sedan began at $2,003, but was capped at $2,475 for the Nova 400 convertible.

With the Chevy II, GM's Chevrolet Division offered a two-fisted approach to the battle of the economy cars. Those who wanted the pleasing and conventional look of a small Chevrolet chose the Chevy II, while the Corvair continued to appeal to those wanting something sporty and unconventional.

Automotive writers enjoyed the Chevy II and said the car was nearly perfect. A Canadian review agreed and summed up the Chevy II this way: "The Chevy II is a sturdy, straightforward utility car which should appeal to the economy-conscious buyer who still wants to enjoy driving."

In the 1962 model year, the Chevrolet strategy was an immediate success. Together, the small Chevrolets sold more than

Canadians also had a slice of the Chevy II pie with the Acadian, a version of the Nova sold only in that country.

144,000 economy models than Ford.

"There's nothing pretentious about the Chevy II," said Canada Track and Traffic in December 1961.

Car Life quickly reminded buyers of the Chevy II's advantages.

"It is sensible, practical, economical basic transportation with the added advantage of full-size interiors, a better ride and a national network of dealers," wrote Car Life reviewers.

One of the few nontraditional elements was found in its rear-spring configuration with long single-leaf, carbon-steel versions in what Chevrolet called the "Mono-Plate design." These mono-leaf springs did not have inner-leaf wear and corrosion problems.

"Extensive Chevrolet testing proved their exceptional durability after tests equivalent to more than 2 million miles," proclaimed Chevrolet writers in promoting the Chevy II. "These springs gave proof of their reliability and superior riding qualities."

The Chevy II was also the first Chevrolet to offer a unitized body and frame combination. That meant less weight. With the Chevy II's entry came the first four-cylinder engine on a Chevy since 1928. It displaced 153 cubic inches and produced 90 hp. The Chevy II six was a 194.4-cid engine that produced 120 hp. Both engines were economical.

There's no doubt that fuel frugality from the Chevy II was the original intention of Chevrolet planners, but the Chevy II was about to launch an evil twin version packing a not-so-efficient V-8 engine. It would forever alter the Chevy II's image, and quickly do so.

CHAPTER 20 — 1962 IMPALA COUPE

Story and photos by Joseph R. Ruth

THANKS MOM!
Sweet '62 Impala stays in the family

The author received this 1962 Chevrolet Impala as a surprise gift from his mother-in-law, who purchased it with low miles from a family friend in the early '80s.

Everybody that loves and enjoys the old car hobby dreams of finding or discovering one of their favorite cars parked and forgotten in an old barn many years ago. That is not the way I acquired my 1962 Impala Sport Coupe.

My wife's parents made a living by operating a small dairy farm in Bucks County, Pa. Since they had 10 children to raise (six boys and four girls), there was never a lot of money left over after the month's bills were paid. With four daughters at home to do the house work, my mother-in-law would clean homes for some of Bucks County's upper class each week to help pay the bills and to give the family a little spending money. Of course, over time, she became good friends with these people.

I believe it was in the early part of the 1980s when my mother-in-law arrived home from one of her cleaning jobs and announced to her husband, "I bought a car today." My father-in-law was surprised, but happy, because they really needed a second car. She told him the car she purchased from one of the families for whom she worked was a 1962 Chevrolet with 30,000 miles. If I remember correctly, she paid $600 for it. Everyone chuckled about the whole thing.

Mom and Dad, as I call my in-laws, really drove the old '62 over the next five to six years. Then I noticed they were starting to use it like a truck! So it was sometime in 1987 when Mom and Dad were at our farm that I casually mentioned to Mom, "I think that Chevy would look really good if it were parked in my barn." Would you believe that several weeks later, Mom and Dad showed up with the car? Mom said she wanted to give me the car — talk about a great mother-in-law! I feel very fortunate to have received the car when she had six sons she could have given it to.

Several years after receiving the car, I removed the front end to remove some rust and dents. I also removed all the trim and the chrome bumpers and polished them. K.B. Godshall in Telford, Pa., completed the body work and painted the car. My wife and I installed reproduction floor carpeting, seat covers and a trunk liner.

Mechanically, the car is original with a 283-cid V-8 and two-barrel carburetor, Powerglide transmission, two-speed wipers, power steering and an AM radio.

The car presently shows 65,000 miles and it rides and drives like a new car. My mother-in-law is still with us, and my wife of 37 years and I enjoy taking the '62 out for a ride every once in a while.

CHAPTER 21 | **1965-69 CORVAIR**

By Byron Olsen

SPORTING CHANCE

The Corvair got an attractive facelift in 1965, but it still faced a difficult battle to survive

Even the four-door Corvair was available only as a sporty hardtop model in the 1965 redesign. This four-door hardtop Sport Sedan is from the Monza series.

The year 1960 was one of significant change for the U.S. automobile industry. For the first time, the major car manufacturers (Ford, Chevrolet and Plymouth) started building two distinctly different sizes of cars. Up to this time, each of these builders had basically said "one size fits all," and buyers had to adjust accordingly. True, there had been high-priced specialty cars like the Corvette and the Thunderbird, but the mainstream sedan and wagon buyers had no choice of size.

And the size had been getting bigger during the late '50s. Detroit was still fixated on a bigger-is-better policy. The problem was, the buying public was disputing this more and more, and showing it by turning to more economical alternatives. During this time, there was a flood of economical imports coming from Europe, led by Volkswagen. These cars were typically small and slow, but reasonably cheap to buy, easy to handle and very economical. Sales of American Motors' Rambler also were booming and would put AMC third place in sales by 1961. The Rambler pitch was the same as the imports: economical and compact (Rambler coined the descriptive word "compact" to describe its product).

The "big three" ignored this as long as

90

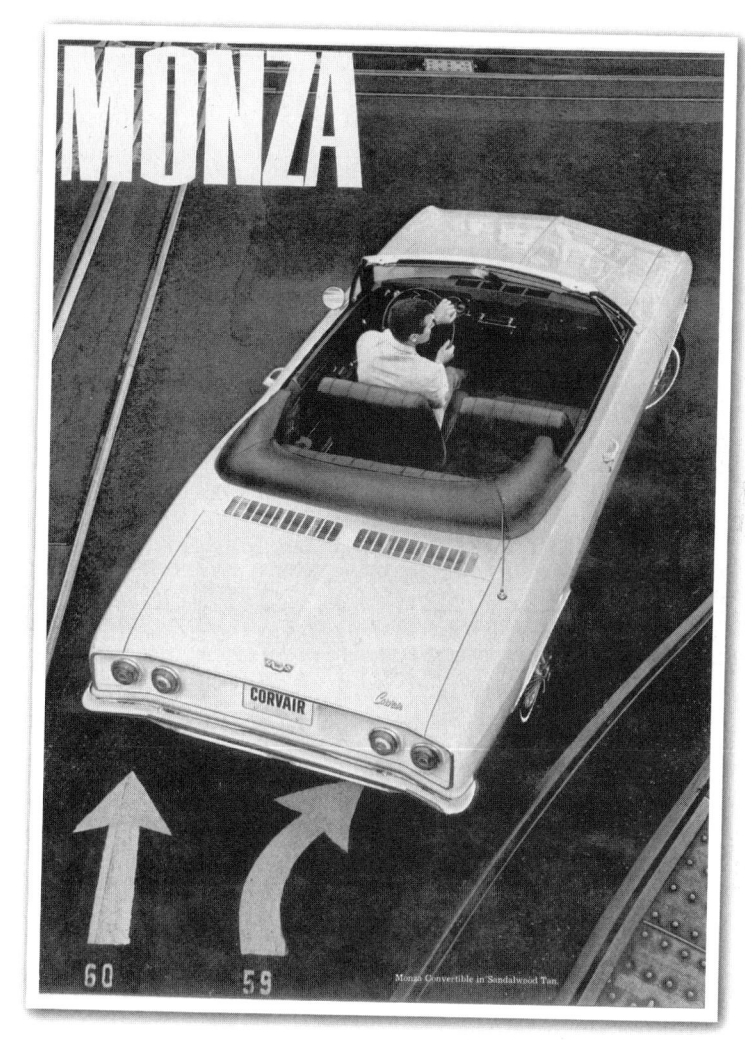

A 1966 Monza convertible is pictured among San Francisco cable car tracks.

they could, but by 1960, something had to be done. The results were three very different answers to the challenge of designing a new small car. Ford, with its Falcon, simply downsized a big car and made the Falcon small, plain, simple, and cheap. It was still front-engine/rear-drive layout and offered no innovative design breakthroughs. The Plymouth response was a bit more interesting. The Valiant appeared with an overhead-valve, slant-six engine and very unusual styling, though still with a front-engine/rear-drive layout.

Chevrolet, on the other hand, took a very innovative approach. Led by Ed Cole, the engineer who led the team that developed the legendary Chevy small-block V-8, took a leaf from the VW design book and put the

The 1965 Corvair Monza convertible listed new for $2,440.

engine in the rear of the new Corvair and air cooled it. This was pretty unusual stuff for the average American car buyer to swallow. Probably only a manufacturer with the market clout of Chevrolet could have made this design sell competitively. The Corvair was small, very economical and handled very easily, because there was no engine weight over the front wheels.

The Falcon was successful from the start, but the Corvair had to work for its sales, partly because of its unusual layout. Other problems developed. The Corvair design did not permit a roomy station wagon, a body type growing rapidly in popularity at this time. Corvair's rear suspension, a single-pivot swing axle similar in concept to what Mercedes-Benz had been using for years, came under fire from Ralph Nader, who was becoming known for his attacks on U.S. car design. Thus, by 1965, when it was time for the first major restyling of the Corvair, GM engineers faced some challenges.

The brilliant result of this effort was the 1965-'69 Corvair. GM took the Corvair in a very sporty direction. The new line offered only hardtops and convertibles. There were no wagons or sedans. The emphasis was on bucket seats, sporty interiors, four-on-the-floor transmissions and other features aimed at motorists who liked European-style sports cars. The lines were beautiful: balanced nicely without trying to look like a front-engine car.

Engine options followed the same sporty trend. All Corvairs used the same displace-

A European-influenced automobile deserves such a rich setting. These new-for-1965 Monzas represent the convertible and Sport Coupe models available that year.

ment, 164-cubic-inch, flat-opposed, air-cooled six-cylinder engine, but horsepower ranged from 95 units in the base models to a 180-bhp turbocharged version in the top-line Corsas. The rear suspension was redesigned with a fully independent trailing arm setup, thus eliminating the source of Nader's criticism. It was truly a family sports car, and a good-looking one at that.

But it was ultimately to no avail. The combination of the unusual design to Americans suspicious of fundamental change in the layout of their cars, coupled with the doubts cast by Nader, were serious problems. Chevrolet had come out with the Chevy II/Nova in 1962 to more directly compete with the Falcon approach to small cars, thus taking another slice of the Corvair market. Then, just before the redesigned Corvair hit the market, the first Mustang came out. It was aimed at the same sporty market as Corvair, but was a more familiar arrangement (front engine/rear drive). Mustang sales really took off just as the revised Corvair tried to get some attention. Still, Corvair sales were pretty good for the 1965 model at 235,528 cars, but then tailed off rapidly. By 1967, the top-line Corsa and turbocharged engine had been dropped, and sales plummeted to 27,253 cars. More competition had arrived in the form of Chevy's own Camaro, another competitor from within. Only 6,000 1969 models were built before production ended.

What is Corvair's legacy? It really started the sporty, colorfully trimmed, bucket-seat craze with the Monza model in 1961. Today, the second-generation Corvairs still look attractive, clean lined and well proportioned. Yet, they can still be purchased for very reasonable prices. It was one of the best examples of a European-style automobile to be built by an American manufacturer. Its size is more consistent with new cars today than the cars of the '60s.

CHAPTER 22 **1966 CHEVELLE**

Story by Gerald Perschbacher

BEST OF BOTH WORLDS

1966 Chevelle could take both quarter miles and curves

Several writers put the 1966 Chevelle Super Sport 396 through its paces when it was new, and every scribe had something noteworthy to say about the car's performance and handling.

"We don't like the idea of a car that goes like a bird when the road's like a ruler, and then turns chicken every time it has to change direction. What's more, we don't think you do, either," said the advertising writer for Chevrolet. His comments were directed at the 1966 Chevelle SS 396. "Be assured, we gave every SS 396 an engine — a 325-hp 396-cubic inch Turbo-jet V-8, with 360 — and 375-hp versions on order. That wasn't all. We gave it suspension, too."

In the 1960s, American car designers and engineers were scurrying to discover the necessity to blend performance and good ride with nimble handling. It wasn't an easy task. Cars made in America were large, by world standards, since America had grown with wide-open spaces and ample-sized city streets — unlike narrow, winding Medieval paths and allies that had become streets and roads in Europe. Sharp curves had not been common to many American byways. But as cars grew faster and more powerful, even the better roads became tricky in high-speed maneuvers. Since the roads could not easily change, carmakers determined to improve their offerings. Hence, the statement by Chevrolet.

What engineers provided for the 1966 Chevelle was simple. "Stiffer coil springs and shocks at all four corners came first," an official explained. "Next, a stiffer anti-sway bar at the front and special frame reinforcements at the back. Then a set of 7.75 x 14 red stripe tires and a fully synchronized three-speed transmission with floor-mounted shift."

The ad writer jumped in: "By the time we were finished, we knew we had your kind of machine; a machine that you could use to demonstrate the techniques of safe precision driving to others." Of course, such a car had to look like speed. So "the final touch was to paint the grille work black and add two businesslike scoops to the hood. After all, this was a machine with a purpose. What we did was give it a purposeful look."

Saying all this didn't make it so. Tests would prove the car's merits.

And tested it was. When the 1966 Chevelle SS 396 bowed, the readers of car magazines hungered for the scoop. Was this truly "a spirited new model from Chevy, designed for those who like to drive?" one auto writer wondered. He was far from alone.

Back then, writer Eric Dahlquist made this observation: "Chevrolet has been kind of out of it the last couple of years, as far as having their own hottest hot dog, but ...guys still remember when she was real fine, that 409," and how those earlier cars were "put back on their heels at the drags in 1961 with their first demonstrations of what a stocker could do."

The 1966 Chevelle speed demon looked different than its ancestor. The sprucing-up was timely, since the first Chevelle tipped its racing helmet in 1963. However, was it moving in the right direction? Those in the know wondered. For 1966, the Chevelle was resembling the full-size Chevrolet more and more.

The earlier version was a little nose-heavy. But for 1966, that was cured, one expert affirmed. This made it a "totally pleasant vehicle, just the ticket for a quiet Sunday drive or drag." Front and rear coil springs were 30 percent heavier than normal, it was reported. There were larger valved-shocks, too. There was a 15/16-inch diameter front sway bar. To avoid cracking, front ball joints were shotpeened.

Some hell-bent drivers of earlier Chevelles had broken rear axles as the reward for performance. It was something they never wanted to "win" again. For 1966, the Chevelle rear housing was more stable when faced with hard use. Wheel hop was under control, compared against the earlier model.

A new reinforcement strut was on the frame between each rear pivot point on upper and lower control arms. The diameter ring gear differential carrier was increased by three-quarters of an inch over the standard dimension.

All business. That's what the changes implied. But there were more. New to any Chevrolet product was an optional all-synchro, heavy-duty, three-speed transmission carrying rations of 2.41, 1.57 and 1.00. Wide, constant-mesh gears were used. Of course, the four-speed was more commonly available. Automatic Powerglide could also be had.

The best test of the Chevelle came from driving. Good as the company-issued reports sounded, and nice as the changes looked when eyeballed by critics, the final nod of success came after road testing.

Under wet driving conditions, the brakes did not receive high marks in 1966. Upon inspection, it was concluded that the shield used by Chevelle to deflect road water was retaining moisture on the brakes. But this was encountered with deep standing pools of water, not the regular course most drivers navigated.

A series of successive stops from 60 mph or greater resulted in brake fade. Some aftermarket improvements could have helped, but most drivers did not intend to put these hot Chevelles to such extreme tests. For drivers in California and the South, welded sintered iron brakes were the answer.

Dick Scritchfield, another automotive tester, commented, "ACTION is the word when you see the Chevelle 396 Super Sport. It LOOKS fast — and on the street or strip, it IS fast!" The 360-hp engine held a high-lift camshaft. A four-barrel carburetor by Holley or Rochester sat atop the masterpiece. The writer said the Holley was better suited for street driving rather than the strip.

Others tested the SS and gave it high marks for speed. One casual run took the car nearly to 98 mph which was considered very respectable for a street equipped stock car. And it felt sturdy to drive, good in handling. In fact, one expert exuberantly lauded the off-the-showroom wonder as having fantastic handling. That was a high honor for a car that could also sub as a daily driver.

The shift mechanism was improved, one tester observed. It was more positive and "goes in every time." That was a step above the four-speed which reportedly threw some fits in fast shifting. But he was worried about the tachometer. It was too close to his right knee. In an accident or a panic stop, the knee or the tach might have been subject to damage.

Another driver testing the SS must have had different knees. The tach was not in danger of being smashed by his knee in radical motion as much as the device could have been the cause of distraction. Located near the floor-mounted shifter, the driver called the position poor. It was not in his line of vision. "If you're using it for racing, you can't be looking down at the floor and hunting around for it when you're going at excess of 60 mph." He opted to move it to the right side of the speedometer since "you don't need the 120 mph area on the street anyway."

To prove the beauty and serious power pent up in the 396 engine, another tester pulled out all the stops. With a stock engine he reached 103 mph in 13.66 seconds. With a slight change in headers and rear gearing, he went to 107 in 13.25 seconds. He ordered experimental cams from the factory and pushed the block to nearly 115 mph in 12.43 seconds. In a subsequent run with larger tires, he dropped that to 12.20 seconds, but it was not recorded as an officially measured achievement.

That 1966 Chevelle SS 396 was a masterpiece in more ways than one. It was lauded in its day. It is revered by those who praise golden achievements in American motoring. It is respected by those who own one today, and by those who wish they did. Is there any greater gauge of success than this?

CHAPTER 23 — **1966 CORVETTE STING RAY**

Story by Bill Holder, photos by Phil Kunz

DREAM MACHINE
Big block Corvette was just too good to pass up

For owner Tom Boyd, there's nothing like dropping the top on his 427-cid-powered 1966 Sting Ray and cruising the town.

Ask Chevy lovers to name the model and engine size of their fantasy performance machine, and more than likely, you are going to hear the same names mentioned. Does the name "Sting Ray" and "427 cubes" sound familiar? Right! It didn't get any better than that in 1966, and they were both available in the same platform: the 427 Sting Ray Corvette.

With a macho design and the muscle car era well under way, the call was boiling for more power under the Corvette's hood, and Chevy answered. Through the 1964 model year, the model showed a maximum displacement of 327 cubes. Other companies' muscle models were powered by en-

When equipped with Chevrolet's snorting 427-cid V-8, the handsome 1966 Corvette Sting Ray not only had panache, it had punch. Boyd's 'Vette carries the desirable knock-off wheels and side exhaust.

gines over 400 cubic inches, and they were kicking butt.

The 1965 response for more power brought big numbers to the table in the form of a 425-horse, 396-cid V-8 big-block. With the so-called "porcupine" heads, the engine was similar to the NASCAR engine used earlier in the decade. Impressive performance was achieved in the quarter-mile, challenging Chrysler's 426-cid Hemi powerhouse.

There had also been talk that the potent 409-cid engine might make a good fit for the company gem. But 'Vette engineer Zora Arkus-Duntov thought the engine would be too heavy for the Vette's stock front suspension.

The lighter 396-cid fit the bill nicely, and with its 11:1 compression ratio, aluminum high-rise intake, solid-lifter cam, four-bolt mains and a 780-cfm Holley carburetor, it was able to make the impressive 425 horsepower figure. You would have thought that performance would have been enough, but Chevrolet was prepared to make the engine even better... and bigger. The 396 was capable of being overbored, and that's exactly what GM did to reach the magic 427 number, which was exactly the same displacement figure that Ford had been using since the early 1960s. Officially, Chevy's 427-cid V-8 was known as the Mark IV 427.

There were two versions of the 427: the L72, which produced 425 horses, and the

390-horse L36. With L72 power in a 3,140-pound machine, the 'Vette's performance was unbelievable. In magazine tests during the period, the L72 Corvette turned 12.8-second quarter-mile times at about 112 mph. The top end was reportedly beyond the 150-mph mark. An interesting sidelight of the engine was that the Corvette brochure indicated that the L72-powered vehicles were for "off-road events" and "not recommended for normal street driving."

Today, Vettes with this powerplant are among the most desirable American-built muscle cars. Only 5,258 of this model were produced, making them not only desirable, but also hard to find after almost 40 years of attrition.

Many 'Vette fans consider the 1966 Sting Ray to be the top Corvette of all, and Tom Boyd of Bellbrook, Ohio, is among those who would agree. When you check out his red-on-red example, you can understand his passion.

Long a vintage Camaro fan, Boyd admitted, "I have loved 'Vettes since I was a kid, but my favorite was always the mid-year 1963-'67 Sting Ray design. I still remember in the late 1970s when a red big-block Sting Ray pulled alongside. I stared at that car and thought, 'That has to be the coolest car of all time.' Finally, in 1999, I decided the time had come for me to buy my dream car, one that I could drive."

Then the story of this car's acquisition becomes real interesting. "After months of searching, I found exactly what I was looking for. I corresponded with the owner in Detroit who agreed to have an NCRS expert check out the machine. He gave a good report, so with a cashier's check in hand, I went to see it and drove it for a test ride.

"It was everything I had dreamed about, but suddenly, for some reason, I got cold feet and decided to pass on it. My wife was astounded on what I did, saying that 'This was exactly the car you always wanted.'"

As soon as he got home, Boyd began to regret his action. But it was too late. When he called the owner, he found out that the car had been sold! Then, depression set in. "How could I let that 'Vette get away?" he asked. The internet search started again, but nothing was found.

"But then I got lucky when I found out that the guy from Mississippi who had bought the car had it up for sale. He found

"It was everything I had dreamed about, but suddenly, for some reason, I got cold feet and decided to pass on it."

out that living without air conditioning down there didn't get it. No air conditioning in these 427 models, you know.

"It didn't take long for me to make the deal and have the car transported back to Ohio. Finally, I had my Rally Red Sting Ray!

"Overall, the car was in excellent shape; the body and frame in outstanding condition. I sent it to the Restoration Station in Springboro, Ohio, to bring it up to the standards I wanted. They were able to locate and install many hard-to-find correct parts, along with rebuilding the engine, replacing some suspension components, and other upgrades."

When it was completed, the new owner indicated that it was too good to drive. "But I got over that, and now it's what I live for. Heck, I get stares, smiles and thumbs-up from passing cars. Looking over the long hood with the high fender arches and big dome hood, listening to the side exhaust sing on a warm summer day... could it get any better?"

The 'Vette is equipped just right, with the M21 close-ratio four-speed manual transmission, teakwood steering wheel, side exhausts, knock-off wheels and an AM-FM radio.

It's red, it's powerful and it's fast. It's a 427 Sting Ray. What else is there to say?

CHAPTER 24 | **1968 CHEVELLE SS RESTORATION**

Story and photos by John Gunnell

A LONG TIME COMING
'68 Chevelle SS is just the "right" restoration project

Keith Cook's spent a long time restoring his '68 SS 396 convertible, but its show record made the job worthwhile.

A person's hobbies can often be traced to his or her memories. A former smoker may collect Zippo lighters and a retired mailman might get into collecting postage stamps.

This story starts out with Keith Cook searching for a new hobby. Cook had happy memories of the good times he had in his teens while working as a mechanic. He also remembered the muscle car he had owned years ago — a blue 1968 Chevelle SS 396 with a white vinyl top and a four-speed gearbox.

Cook decided to get involved in the car-collecting hobby and started searching for a restoration project. He considered and rejected several cars. He felt that a Pontiac GTO was too hard to find. A Corvette was too expensive. Ultimately, another Chevelle seemed to be a good choice.

In January of 1995, the "right" car turned up in a classified ad. It was a maroon 1968 Chevelle convertible with the L34 version of the 396-cid engine, Turbo Hydra-Matic transmission and a white convertible top. Cook called about the car right away. Unfortunately, he could not come to an agreement with the owner on a mutually acceptable price.

Cook spent a lot of time researching the correct features of the 350-hp L34 option to ensure that his Chevelle was properly restored. Joining a club, judging other cars and buying all related books are some of his recommendations.

Cook decided to look at the car anyway. He liked it and decided he certainly wanted to own a Chevelle. He joined the National Chevelle Owners' Association so he could learn more about the market. He attended the club's national Chevelle show in June of that year.

"What a sight the show cars were," Cook remembers. "I liked what I saw and started asking what the value of the maroon convertible might be." Cook was a bit crushed by the responses he got and felt he could never afford the car of his dreams.

About a week after the show, the phone rang. The car's widowed owner said she was going to sell it and her future husband's hot rod at an upcoming auction. "I told her I would be there," says Cook . "But I warned her that it might not be in her best interest not to sell at auction and offered to up my previous offer by a final $1,000." The lady called the next day and said that she would take Cook's offer. He arranged for a car hauler and picked it up that weekend.

Even though the car's engine had been overhauled before the woman's husband died, Cook had to unbolt the fuel pump and hook a hose to a gas can to start the Chevelle. Then, he ran it on the car hauler and tied it down, paid the money and started home.

The car was unloaded and Cook started tearing it down the next day. He took pictures and tagged everything he took off. After two weeks, the woman Cook bought the car from called. She had told her son about selling the car and he wanted to buy it back for $3,000 more than Cook paid for it, even though it was torn down, with the parts stored in boxes. Cook considered the offer, but decided to keep it.

Cook spent the next 12 years on his restoration project. There were experiences and expenses that held up working on the car, such as his kids getting married and having to tear down his old barn and erect a steel building. He had to keep setting money aside for the project, too.

After "plugging away" for many years, in April 2007, Cook told his wife that the car would be finished in a couple of weeks. That June, he took the Chevelle to its first car show, which was a Chevelle club national meet. Amazingly, it placed in the top three cars. He then took it to an NCOA Ohio Regional Meet where it again placed in the top three cars. The car placed well in three local car shows, too. Then, it copped a Gold Spinner Award at the Chevy VetteFest in Rosemont, Ill.

Cook is happy with the recognition the car has earned and is willing to share the factors that he feels made his project a success.

"In my opinion, joining the National Chevelle Owners' Association and taking advantage of the opportunity to start judging at their events was a critical step," says Cook. "The first year I was trained under five very knowledgeable judges. Then, I was able to judge for the next three or four years and it was a learning experience."

When Cook started the restoration, the body men he hired told him to have the frame and body acid dipped, so that every nook and cranny of the car was cleaned of rust and debris. He then followed their advice to have the parts E-coated and powder coated and to have the body E-coated after the body panels were replaced. "I assembled most of the body myself," Cook points out. "But anything I was not a professional at had to be hired done, although I helped out wherever I could."

Cook bought every 1968 Chevelle service manual and assembly manual that he could find. "The information in these books ended up helping out my mechanic, body man and especially me," he notes.

"I have to admit that researching what is right and wrong for a car and hunting down parts all over the country was just as challenging as the assembly work itself," says Cook. "At the first year national Chevelle show we attended, I found a chart put out by Team Chevelle that shows the production numbers on about every Chevelle and factory option produced between 1964 and 1972. It indicates that only 126 of these 1968 Chevelle SS 396, 350-hp Turbo Hydra-Matic convertibles were made."

Armed with the production totals for his car and options array, Cook had his Chevelle professionally appraised for insurance purposes. His appraiser valued it higher than he ever imagined. "This restoration project has been one of the most rewarding experiences of my life," says Cook. "But, restoration is also humbling because it is such a challenge."

CHAPTER 25 — 1968 CHEVELLE SS

By Brian Earnest

FAMILY JEWEL

Like many Chevelles, this beloved 1968 SS 396 has done it all

Larry Sebranek's Butternut Yellow 1968 Chevelle SS 396 has served many roles, from family hauler to drag car to trailer queen. Sebranek bought the car new, eventually sold it, then tracked it down and bought it back in 1996. Today it is a fully restored gem.

Larry Sebranek's 1968 Chevelle SS 396 is one of those cars that's lived a very full life. It started off as Vietnam vet's dream car, went on to ably serve as a mean street machine terrorizing the Wisconsin backroads, eventually became a grocery getter and all-around family hauler, then changed owners and started collecting pink slips at the drag strip.

Then, back in 1996, it was sold back to its original owner, Sebranek, of Lone Rock, Wis., who has happily turned his beloved Chevy muscle car into a fully restored and appropriately pampered trailer queen.

Sebranek's stellar SS 396 is proof, once again, that you can do a lot with a Chevelle — a true muscle car for the masses.

"It was our family car for, I betcha, eight, nine, 10 years," Sebranek said. "It had kids in it, crackers on the floor, the whole deal. You didn't really think about it back then. It was the grocery getter. I hauled my wife

Sebranek's Chevelle came new with some unique interior items and upholstery that he eventually figured out came from the Buick Gran Sport. A short-term labor dispute at GM resulted in some 1968 Chevelles getting GS interior pieces.

and kids to and from the hospital. Back then, it was just a car.

"I bought it brand new when I came home from Vietnam. It's got the 396 (-cubic-inch), 375-horse engine it. I ordered it when I came home from leave. When we were over there we got a lot of brochures on muscle cars ... I wanted a 427 and the dealer said, 'You can't get it, we'll get you a 396.' I was naive and didn't know, and you believe what the dealer said, you know? So, the first one came in and had the 396 and 325 horse. I said, 'No, that's not the one I want.'

"I remember my dad calling me and saying, 'What the hell you want that big motor for?' I said, 'That's the one I want!'"

Eventually, another SS came in, but Sebranek turned that one down, too. Finally, a third 396 came to the dealer and it had something unique about it. "The interior was always different, but nobody could really tell me what the interior was," he said. "The dealer said, 'Well, somebody must have screwed up.' I was a young kid and didn't really know, so I took it, and it was finally about 10 years later that I found out it was a Buick Gran Sport interior ... Apparently, GM was on strike, or something, and some Chevelles got the Gran Sport interiors. You'd get different stories over the years, and yet there is no official record of GM being on strike. But there are a few cars out there like this that got the Gran Sport interior. The guys who really know Chevelles know about them ... There's no logos, no 396 logos on doors, the seats are completely different in a '68 Chevelle. A Buick guy could probably pick it out right away. The Gran Sport has more of a pleated upholstery in it."

Sebranek loved his Chevelle – the first new car he had ever purchased — and he had some painful seller's remorse from the moment he sold it to a man in Texas more than 20 years ago.

"In about '87, we sold it. Our son was getting old enough to drive, and I just had raised enough hell with that car that I knew what it would do and I knew how dangerous it was for a 16-year-old boy," Sebranek said. "I hated to see it go, but then you know, when you got two boys and one's getting old enough to drive, it's hard to say no to them. I would have had to say 'no' 100 percent of the time. That was dad's car.

"About six months after I sold it, I started tracking it. At that time you could call the DMV and, if you gave them $5 or $10, they could tell you who owned it ... So I knew who had the car."

Sebranek eventually worked up the nerve to contact the second owner to ask if he could buy the car back, but the man de-

> *"Oh, I never thought I'd get it back. Words can't describe that telephone call. When he asked, 'Do you want to buy it back?' it was probably one of the happiest days that Judy and I ever had."*

clined. "I kind of gave up on it after that," he said.

But he got one more chance. About five years later, the man sent a letter to Sebranek asking some questions about a warranty block that had been put in the car when it had 48,000 miles on the odometer. "I asked him again if he wanted to sell it. He called me a week later and said he'd sell it back to me. He lived in Kentucky at the time, so we grabbed a trailer and a come-along and we used a winch and went and got it.

"It had been a wrecked a little bit. The right front was dinged up and had quite a bit of mud (body filler) in it. And there was mud all over the wheel wells. It was done in sort of a cobbled fashion. The driver's seat was torn. But for the average Joe, it was still a good car for being that old."

During its time away, the Chevelle hadn't been hauling many kids or groceries. "It had been a drag car," Sebranek said. "The guy had it to Pomona [Calif.]. He even showed me the slips with the times it had run."

The fact that it was a street-and-strip demon certainly didn't hurt the wildly popular 1968 Chevelle in the eyes of the buying public when the cars were new. The muscle engines started with the base SS engine, a 396-cid big-block V-8 with 325 hp. Two more-powerful versions were optional. The 325- and 350-hp versions of the 396-cid V-8 were available with a special heavy-duty, three-speed Synchromesh transmission mounted on the floor as standard equipment. A four-speed manual gearbox and Powerglide or Turbo Hydra-Matic automatic transmissions were optional. The 375-hp versions, which had to be special ordered, and there was usually a two- to three-month waiting period to get one.

The high-performance SS 396 was a separate series in 1968. It included a sport coupe base-priced at $2,899 and a convertible priced at $3,102. Both had the shorter wheelbase, of course. Overall length, at 197.1 inches, was just a tad longer than in 1967, even though the wheelbase was downsized by three inches. Front and rear tread widths were also up an inch to 59 inches. The new Chevelle was also nearly an inch taller at 52.7 inches.

The SS 396 models were made even more distinctive by the use of a matte black finish around the full lower perimeter of the bodies, except when the cars were finished in a dark color. Other standard SS 396 features included F70 x 14 wide-oval red-stripe tires, body accent stripes, a special twin-domed hood with simulated air intakes, "SS" badges and vinyl upholstery.

For '68, the "flying buttress" roofline of the Chevelle sport coupe was replaced by a more fastback style and the rear windows had a "V" appearance (also used on pillared coupes). The round-lens head-lamps were placed in square, hooded chrome housings that edged up into the hood line.

As in the past, Chevrolet continued to offer the SS 396 with a wide range of transmission and rear axle options. Also standard were finned front brake drums and new bonded brake linings all around. About 57,600 Chevelle SS 396s were made, and this total included 4,751 with the L78 (375-hp) engine and 4,082 with the L34 (350-hp) option. The L35 code denoted the base 325-hp SS 396.

Sebranek had no plans to race his Chevelle once he got it back. And he wasn't going to be hauling groceries, either. The Chevelle went on to get a full restoration, courtesy of Newton's Restorations and Al's Interiors, both of Spring Green, Wis.

"Oh, I never thought I'd get it back," Sebranek said. "Words can't describe that telephone call. When he asked, 'Do you want to buy it back?' it was probably one of the happiest days that Judy and I ever had."

The restoration started in 2001 and took more than two years. The car now makes occasional appearances at shows, and is occasionally taken for gentle weekend drives – a far cry from its former lives as a bachelor street racer, kid transporter, and then drag car.

"You don't realize how stupid we were, to put it plainly," Sebranek said, of his crazy younger days when he drove his Chevelle with a heavy foot. "Now, honestly, I'm scared now to drive it over 60 mph. We've got the bias-ply tires on it. When I was young, I had that car in third gear at 120 mph. Before I was married, I used to do my share of street racing, and it was a tough car to beat. And I enjoyed every minute of it, but you don't realize how safe our tires are compared to the old tires we had. It's just completely different worlds.

"The guys who restored the car just did an unbelievable job. We've had it to shows and won some awards. We just won 'Best Paint' and 'Best Engine' at the Iowa Falls show.

"It's a Butternut Yellow, so it's not an eye-catcher. To the average guy it's just a car, but guys who know paint, who know cars, and who know Chevelles, they know it's a helluva car."

CHAPTER 26 | 1969 FRED GIBB CAMARO

By John Gunnell

DEALING IN SPEED

Legendary Chevy dealer Fred Gibb put plenty of muscle behind the Camaro, and the drag racers he sponsored

Fred Gibb (second from left) sponsored Dickie Harrell's ZL-1 Camaro Unlimited Fuel car, which set quarter-mile marks as low as 7.35 seconds at 209 mph.

Fred Gibb came to firmly believe that "what wins on Sunday sells on Monday," so he saw racing as a way to boost sales. He didn't realize that his involvement would eventually make his name famous among muscle car collectors, nor could he have predicted his interest in going fast would lead to the development of a legendary automobile — the 1969 ZL-1 Camaro.

Old Cars Weekly met Helen Gibb, Fred's widow, at the Nickey Muscle Car and Corvette Nationals in Rosemont, Ill., Nov. 21-22, 2009. Stefano Bimbi, of Nickey Chicago, had arranged for Helen to be in his booth with her original Fred Gibb Nova. She also brought along the Gibb family racing photo album and shared several photographs from the storied dealership's past.

Fred Gibb was a Chevrolet dealer who opened shop in the small western Illinois town of La Harpe, in 1948. According to Helen, Fred wasn't always involved in drag racing. His interest in the sport started in

Above, Jim Hayter (right) campaigned a ZL-1 Camaro for Fred Gibb Chevrolet. Right, High-performance legend Fred Gibb (right) stands outside his famous Chevrolet dealership in La Harpe, Ill.

1967 when one of his best salesmen — a man named Herb Fox — ordered a 1967 Camaro Z/28 and started racing it. Before long, Fred caught the racing bug, too.

When it all started in June 1967, the Z/28 package wasn't very well-known. Fox ordered a Royal Plum (purple) Z/28 with white racing stripes. His car had the standard black interior and a black vinyl top. He had a man who painted DOT signs on trucks letter the Camaro for racing. It was nicknamed "Little Hoss" — a

Because of their rarity, tremendous horsepower and relatively low weight, the Fred Gibb and other COPO 9560 ZL-1 Camaros are now considered perhaps the quickest and most valuable Camaros ever built.

play on the character of Hoss Cartwright from the Chevy-sponsored "Bonanza" TV show and a poke at Ford's "pony car" — the Mustang.

For the 1968 season, Fred Gibb painted "Little Hoss" a bright red color and installed a set of Corvette knock-off wheels. Fox raced the car all over the United States. Helen recalled that once on the road, the racing team had to keep moving and rarely even stopped at rest stops. The car became the 1968 American Hot Rod Association World Championship winner. At an awards banquet in Kansas City, Fred Gibb and Fox picked up a lot of brass. "Little Hoss" was the Top Stock points leader for 1968 and the nation's winningest Chevrolet.

By 1968, Fred Gibb Chevrolet was performing engine swaps for customers interested in racing. That same year, the dealership used Chevrolet's Central Office Production Order (COPO) system to order 50 special Nova models with 396-cid/375-hp V-8s and experimental Turbo-Hydra-Matic transmissions. These cars became known as COPO 9738 Novas. Some of them were later converted into 427-cid Supercars.

It was in 1969 that Gibb became instrumental in the development of the aluminum-block ZL-1 Camaro. The idea to develop the ZL-1 grew out of Gibb's close friendship with Chevy high-performance guru Vince Piggins. The two men actually conceived the ZL-1 idea, and Piggins told Gibb he should utilize the COPO system to order 50 cars with factory-installed aluminum-block 427s.

Chevrolet brass liked the idea, but wouldn't grant approval unless it had a dealer commitment to sell at least 50 cars. Gibb assured GM that he could sell the 50 cars himself at a projected price of $4,900 and the cars were quickly built.

The first two Dusk Blue ZL-1 COPO 9560 Camaros were delivered to Gibb on Dec. 31, 1968. They were exactly as specified. The day the first ZL-1s arrived, it was 22 degrees below zero in La Harpe. One car would not start on such a cold day, so a tow truck was used to pull it off the transporter. Forty-eight additional ZL-1s were delivered to Gibb in March 1969. However, there was a major problem. The sticker price was not $4,900, but a rather startling $7,269, or about twice as much as a COPO 9561 Camaro with the cast-iron 427.

The higher price was due to a new GM policy specifying that the company would no longer absorb most research and development costs associated with specialty vehicles. Instead, they were incorporated into the dealer cost of the car. This raised the cost of the COPO 9560 option from about $400 to $4,000.

Gibb knew that it was very unlikely that he could sell all 50 Camaros at a $7,000-plus price. He was actually able to sell just 13 of the ZL-1 cars. He convinced Chevrolet to take 37 of the cars back, re-invoice them and re-distribute them to other high-performance dealers. This may have been the first time the factory had ever allowed a dealer to return cars. Eventually, the other dealers sold all the cars and ordered an additional 19 units. This resulted in a total production run of 69 ZL-1s.

There was also a plan to produce a batch of 100 COPO 9567 ZL-1 Camaros for street use. This "ZL-1 Special Camaro" (as GM paperwork called it) was Piggins' baby. It was to include Tuxedo Black paint with special gold striping, a de-tuned 427 with an 11.0:1 compression ratio and other equipment. Piggins and his staff hand-built two prototypes — one four-speed and one with a Turbo Hydra-Matic — to show executives and to street race.

Because of their rarity, tremendous horsepower and relatively low weight, the Fred Gibb and other COPO 9560 ZL-1 Camaros are now considered the quickest and most valuable Camaros ever built.

Dickie Harrell — who became the driver of one of Gibb's own ZL-1 Camaros drag cars — started racing when he was 14 years old. After a three-year stint in the U.S. Army, he got back into racing and by the mid '60s, he was traveling all over the country to race. In 1965, he went to work for Nickey Chevrolet. After a couple years, he started his own performance shop in St. Louis, Mo.

In 1967, Harrell had started working with Fred Gibb on the "Little Hoss" car and also worked with Don Yenko when the Pennsylvania dealer was engineering his Yenko Super Camaro. Harrell continued to work with Gibb and helped him take the ZL-1 to the Nationals. His car ran in the Unlimited Fuels class. As a result, La Harpe became known as the home of the top Super Stock drag racing cars. By January 1969, the dealership was preparing its own Super Stock racing car. It was Candy Apple Red and had the Fred Gibb emblem on the door. The car was first raced at the Winternationals in Phoenix, where it ran strong against the factory-backed cars of Sox & Martin and Don Groether.

The car traveled across country on a specially built Chevrolet truck that was painted white and fitted with a custom body made

Gibb got into racing when his top salesman. Herb Fox, purchased a '67 Camaro Z/28 and began to drag race.

in Texas. It had 1,000-gallon gas tanks so the crew could skip gas stations and those pesky rest stops. The car was hauled more than 25,000 miles that year. As the team was booked for races further away from home, Ray Sullins replaced Fox and did most of the driving.

The Super Stock car beat the class record in AHRA competition. It turned in performances such as a 10.05-second quarter-mile time at 139 mph. Harrell's Unlimited Fuel car looked basically identical to the Super Stock Camaro, but was faster, of course. It set times as low as 7.35 seconds at 209 mph. Harrell — who was known as "Mr. Chevrolet" and "Mr. Reflexes" — won at the AHRA Winternationals, the NHRA Winternationals and the World Championship in Ft. Worth, Texas. He was considered the top funny car driver of the day.

Harrell died in a racing accident in 1971. Fred Gibb continued running his dealership until he sold it in 1984. He died in 1994, but his legacy remains with people collecting the actual cars he created or building clones of them. According to Bimbi, a genuine Camaro ZL-1 is worth at least $1 million today. Helen says the nicest thing is that everyone who knew Gibb respected him for his accomplishments and his outstanding character.

CHAPTER 27 | **1969 CAMARO Z/28**

Story and photos by John Gunnell

CRA-Z

A wild '69 Camaro Z/28 built to little-known Chevrolet 'service component' racing specs

After doing his homework, Guy Carpenter ordered this 1969 Camaro Z/28 exactly the way he wanted it when he was only 19. He had it tuned every Friday morning so he could race it over the weekend. He put 15,000 miles on it in 1969, but has added only 692 miles since.

Guy Carpenter of Marshfield, Wis., has been a car enthusiast since he was in high school. As a teenager, he read all the car magazines and spent a lot of time hanging around Wheeler Chevrolet, his hometown Chevy dealer.

Carpenter grew up in the muscle car era and knew a lot about cars — Chevrolets, in particular. In fact, by the age of 19, he knew exactly what car he wanted, what color it

Originally, the car was delivered new without a rear deck lid spoiler, which was in short supply in January 1969. Another Z/28 came in the same day without a spoiler. The parts were shipped to the dealer and installed later on.

should be, what regular production options he wanted on it and what "factory" performance upgrades he wanted to make it go faster.

Like many young enthusiasts of the time, Carpenter was in love with the "shark" Corvette that arrived in 1968. He wanted to buy a big-block version, but his father warned him about the exorbitant insurance.

With his knowledge of Chevy muscle cars, Carpenter also knew everything about the Z/28 Camaro with its race-bred small-block V-8. As he suspected, its 302-cid V-8 was the only thing his insurance agent looked at to determine an affordable rate,

so the astute teenager started looking for a LeMans Blue Z/28 with go-fast option content, rather than luxury extras.

An uncle who lived in southern Wisconsin located a LeMans Blue '68 Z/28 RS at Humphrey Chevrolet in Janesville. It even had the white body stripes and optional wood-grained Sport steering wheel that Carpenter was looking for, although the radio and Custom interior weren't really on his "want" list. The car was a little more money than Carpenter had, but the biggest thing against it was that he hadn't ordered it to his specifications. He did not want a car off the dealer's lot.

Shortly after, the dealer in Marshfield invited Carpenter to sit in on a training program to see the 1969 models. When he saw the '69 Z/28 Rally Sport model, he was immediately hooked. He was excited about the addition of optional four-wheel disc brakes and the fact that the Z/28's 302-cid V-8 had been updated with floater wrist pins, four-bolt mains and other racing enhancements.

Carpenter and Wheeler Chevrolet salesman Al Burris wrote the order, specifying a Z/28 hardtop with the M-22 gearbox, four-wheel disc brakes, rosewood steering wheel, Rally Sport goodies, the lighter-weight base interior — a car exactly the way he wanted.

The order was placed on the first date that Chevrolet's Zone Office would take orders for '69 models. Shortly afterwards, Wheeler Chevrolet was notified that four-wheel disc brakes weren't available. Would Carpenter take the car without them? Nope! The order went in again and came back the same way, so Carpenter had it re-entered. Chevrolet didn't have things ready to go on the cars until December, when Carpenter's re-order for a car with disc brakes finally was accepted. Carpenter's car — the exact one he ordered — came in late January.

The engine was converted to Trans-Am racing specifications in the 1970s using GM service component parts. These were ordered off the old "green sheets" issued by Chevrolet to help enthusiasts turn Camaros and 'Vettes into race cars.

From the day he picked it up, Carpenter knew he was going to keep his Z/28 forever. It arrived on a snowy day, so he stored it until the spring of 1969. Then, he got rid of the smog equipment and added a set of tuned headers and put the car on the road. Over the next few months, he put 15,000 miles on it. At that rate, it seemed he would have a hard time keeping it forever, but he still has the Z/28 — and now it only has 15,692 miles. Yes, since the fall of 1969, Carpenter has added only 692 miles of use. Today, the car looks brand new, still has all of its factory markings and has never had a lick of restoration. However, the car has received some very special factory-offered upgrades.

Did we mention Carpenter likes racing? That first summer, he street raced the car and always did well. The race-bred Z/28 loved highways and hated towns. The plugs would sometimes foul during his daily travels around town, so Carpenter often drove to towns 40-50 miles away to "blow out the carbon." A talented mechanic at Wheeler Chevrolet installed a Mallory dual-point distributor that allowed the 302 engine to wind up well over 7,000 rpm. Carpenter had that mechanic tune the car every Friday morning so it was ready to blow doors off other competitors over the weekend.

The Camaro's interior looks new. Carpenter still has all factory documents for the car, two copies of the magazine with the article that inspired his racing upgrades and photos from the day that the car came in at Wheeler Chevrolet in January 1969.

On many weekends, Carpenter drove hundreds of miles to the drag strip in Kaukauna, Wis., or road races at Elkhart Lake. He visited his uncle in Janesville and his brother in Illinois. Other times, he drove to a buddy's cabin near Minocqua. Carpenter wanted to enjoy the car that summer as it came from the factory, then perform some special modifications, but then he got his draft notice in July and entered the U.S. Army on Sept. 8. He was able to drive the car until November, but then had to store it for three years.

While in the service, Carpenter thought about what he wanted to do to the car. While he had waited for the car to come in, he read a story called "Trans-Am Racers For The Road" in the July 1968 issue of Car and Driver. It compared a Z/28 and a Mustang that were both equipped with factory-issued Trans-Am racing hardware, including cross-ram intakes for multi-carburetion, as well as other special racing components. Carpenter decided to search for all the factory parts needed to convert his Camaro to be like the Z/28 in that article.

In the late '60s, Chevrolet put out mimeographed "green sheets" that listed the numbers of the parts needed to modify a Camaro or Corvette for racing. Carpenter

"I enjoy the car, but, it's not something I use like I did at 19."

had the sheets. After he was discharged in the fall of 1971, he went back to Wheeler Chevrolet to order the parts. Unfortunately, that was a time when the muscle car era was winding down and many of the parts he wanted were long gone. While he was able to get a few of the parts from the dealership needed to convert his Z/28 into what Chevrolet called a "service component" car, he could not get other important parts, such as the cross-ram manifold.

In 1976, Carpenter saw an interesting classified ad in a hobby magazine. It advertised several Trans-Am components, including a special hemi-head 302 that had never been put into production. Carpenter responded to the ad and asked if they might have other Trans-Am parts. The man said that he had purchased race car builder Smokey Yunik's parts and had a complete cross-ram setup for a 1968-'69 Trans-Am Camaro. After waiting so long, Carpenter didn't question the asking price. He simply asked how quickly the seller could have it crated and shipped to Wisconsin.

Once Carpenter had all the Trans-Am parts, his Z/28 was taken apart and re-assembled according to the "green sheets" that provided the power train and chassis specifications that Chevy engineers had worked out for racing cars. With the Trans-Am goodies, the car was no longer suited for everyday street use, since it ran like a race car. It has been driven only 140 miles in its current build.

"I enjoy the car," Carpenter says. "But, it's not something I use like I did at 19."

And just like he did at 19, Carpenter recently returned to Wheeler Chevrolet with his Camaro. On this occasion, however, the Camaro was present to promote the first 2010 Camaro the dealership received.

CHAPTER 28 / 1969 CORVETTE

Story and photos by John Gunnell

THE 'EXCEPTION'

Menacing, fast and cool, the '69 'Vette was the real deal

This dark green 1969 Corvette coupe with removable roof panels and the L88 engine was photographed while on display at Bloomington Gold in St. Charles, Illinois. The '69s continued with the same swoopy styling introduced in 1968, but they were definitely not the same car.

"With the one beautiful exception, there is no such thing as a true American sports car," said one advertisement for the '69 Corvette.

Then, Chevy somewhat contradicted itself by teaming the 'Vette and Camaro in another ad that read, "We'll take on any two other cars in the magazine." The Camaro, the Mustang, the Barracuda and the AMX were all sporty cars, but the '69 'Vette was truly the answer to any question over whether America had a real sports car.

Late in 1967, my boss purchased the first 1968 Corvette sold in the state of New Jersey. It was a white convertible with a tan interior, a black top and a 427-cid big-block V-8. It was a sports car. It was good looking, fast and exciting. So what if it was in the repair shop almost every other week? Chevy hadn't worked all of the bugs out of the car in '68, but once again, the '69 was different.

In 1969, the Corvette's back-up lights were integrated into the center of the inner taillights. This is the view many driver's of other cars got of the big-block '69 Corvette.

The 1969 Corvette had numerous improvements over the first edition of the "sharks." True, it continued to feature the swoopy styling introduced in 1968, but it was not the same car. A new grille with black-finished bars replaced the chrome grille of 1968. The Corvette's interior was also roomier, and the base V-8 was stroked to 3.48 inches to increase displacement to 350 cubic inches.

After disappearing in 1968, the sexy Sting Ray name reappeared on the 1969 Corvette. However, it was now spelled as one word — "Stingray." Badges on the front fenders, above four slanting vents, carried the new name.

The Corvette's back-up lamps were now integrated into the center of the inner tail lamps. A steering-column-mounted ignition switch was used and the exterior door buttons used on '68 models disappeared in favor of cleaner-looking, key-operated locks. There were other small changes, such as the wheel rims growing from seven inches wide to eight inches wide in order to improve the car's handling characteristics. The steering wheel shrunk from 16 inches to 15, making the car easier to enter. A stiffer frame eliminated shaking.

Inside the car, the interior was a bit roomier. The door panels were mildly redesigned. They now had a thicker upper section and a horizontally mounted handle. Standard Corvette equipment included four-wheel disc brakes, headlight washers, a central convenience console, wheel trim rings, floor carpeting and all-vinyl upholstery.

The 350-cid V-8 became the base small-

The wheel rims grew from seven inches wide to eight inches wide for 1969 in order to improve the car's handling characteristics.

block offering this year starting with 300 hp in a mild hydraulic-lifter four-barrel format. RPO L46 was the hotter version with 11.0:1 compression and one horsepower per cubic inch. Since this was getting into the heavy-duty, muscle era, there were no less than six 427s available in the 'Vette, either as a regular or special option.

The 427-cid 390-hp RPO L36 V-8 was again the starting-point engine for muscle car enthusiasts. Then came RPO L68. It was the same 10.25:1 compression V-8 fitted with three two-barrel carburetors, which upped its output to 400 hp. The 427-cid/435-hp RPO L71 Tri-Power engine also returned in much the same form as 1968.

Three ultra-high-performance options began with the RPO L88 V-8. Hot Rod tested an L88 and described it as a "street machine with soul." This year, the basic L88 package required heavy-duty brakes and suspension, transistor ignition and Positraction. An L88 convertible with a beefy Turbo Hydra-Matic and 3.36:1 rear axle could do the quarter-mile in 13.56 seconds at 111.10 mph.

There was also the RPO L89 V-8. This was a solid-lifter version of the 427 with aluminum heads on the L71 block. It had a 12.0:1 compression ratio and developed 435 hp at 5,800 rpm. The L89 produced a hefty

"Stingray." Badges were carried on the front fenders, above the four slanting air vents.

460 lbs.-ft. of torque at 4,000 rpm.

Also available in 1969 was a 427 that was possibly the wildest performance muscle engine ever offered to the public until recent times. This RPO ZL1 all-aluminum big-block V-8 was installed in 69 Camaros and only two production Corvettes. About 10-12 Corvette engineering test "mules" were also built with ZL1s. They were used in magazines, engineering tests and track evaluations and driven by the likes of Zora Arkus-Duntov and GM VIPs. The evaluation vehicles were all destroyed. However, two 'Vettes went out the door as ZL1s — a Canary Yellow car with side pipes and a Can-Am white T-top coupe with black ZL1 side stripes.

ZL1 was technically an optional version of the L88 engine, but it was some option with its thicker walls and main webbing and dry-sump lubrication provisions. The bottom end had four-bolt main bearings, a forged-steel crank, rods with 7/16-inch bolts, Spiralock washers and full floating pins. The pistons had a higher dome than the L88 type and boosted compression to 12.5:1. The cylinder heads were also aluminum and featured open combustion chambers, round exhaust ports and 2.19-inch/1.88-inch valves. The aluminum dual plane intake was topped by an 850-cfm Holley "double-pumper" four-barrel carburetor featuring mechanical secondaries. The ZL1's radical solid-lifter camshaft allowed the engine to stay together in the upper revs range.

Car Life magazine wrote, "Corvettes are for driving, by drivers... The Corvette driver will be tired of smiling long before he's tired of the car." Corvette buyers backed that view by ordering 38,762 cars. That was over 10,000 more cars than they had purchased in 1968.

CHAPTER 29 — 1970 CORVETTE

Story and photos by John Gunnell

FOREVER BLUE
Restorer's 'Blue Hawaii' 'Vette holds four decades worth of memories

Dennis Bickford's 1970 T-top Corvette has the 350-cid V-8 and a four-speed manual gearbox. Today the Corvette is not used much, but it is carefully stored to preserve it.

In the 1961 film "Blue Hawaii," Chad Gates (played by rock 'n' roll legend Elvis Presley) has just gotten out of the U.S. Army and is tickled pink to be back in Hawaii with his surf board and his beach buddies. The romantic movie revolved around dancing, singing and partying in one of the world's lushest paradises. The Elvis song "Can't Help Falling in Love" was a by-product of this bouncy flick and took awards for being the most-performed big-screen tune of its time.

Dennis Bickford's Hawaiian experience also had something to do with the military, but it involved his being in the U.S. Air Force, and the only tune being sung was the exhaust note from his 1970 "Blue Hawaii" Corvette as he and his wife, Kathy, cruised the highways of Honolulu in their "shark" car.

This 'Vette has a removable rear window and a luggage rack.

Today, the Bickfords restore woodies for a living. Their shop in Iola, Wis., is internationally known for fabricating factory-correct wooden panels for Classic Chrysler Town and Countrys made just after World War II, as well as complete restorations of the cars. In the past few years, Dennis and Kathy have added a reproduction parts manufacturing business that keeps them very busy making Chrysler and Plymouth parts for cars of the same era. Still, every once in awhile, the Bickfords get out their 1970 Chevrolet Corvette Stingray, because it brings back memories of the good old days.

Dennis purchased the Corvette in 1970 in Honolulu. "We weren't the first owners," he admitted. "It was sold brand new by Aloha Motors and belonged to a Hawaiian fellow who was a real family man."

The man thought the car was fun to own, but felt it was not made for his family. When the Bickfords married, the newlyweds did not need a family car. "The 'Vette was only about five months old when we got it," Dennis recalled.

Shortly after he purchased the Corvette, Bickford added a locking gas cap to the car, but doing so had nothing to do with people pilfering fuel during a gas crunch. He says that Hawaiian gas pump jockeys had a bad habit of sliding the cap across the deck when they removed it to add gas to the tank. To avoid getting scratches in the paint, Dennis first put a sign on the cap that read, "Do Not Remove Under Penalty of Death." When the sign didn't do much good, he bought the locking gas cap.

Since Bickford was with the U.S. Air Force in Hawaii, the military sent the car back home after his tour of duty was up.

"We were waiting to pick the Corvette up at U.S. Customs in San Francisco, Calif. We got worried when it didn't come through and other people's cars did," Dennis said. "Then a customs agent came out and asked us where the Corvette's battery was."

On a '70 Stingray, the battery is located in a compartment behind the seat. The battery had gone dead and the officials had no luck finding where General Motors mounted it. They eventually got the Corvette started, but once they did, Dennis worried about the car being stolen while it was near the Port of Entry in San Diego. As he slept in a relative's home that night, he tied a string from the Corvette, ran it through the bedroom window and tied the other end around his big toe so he would wake up if the car took off.

It was warm in San Diego, but by the time Dennis and Kathy reached Chicago on their way back to Wisconsin, the temperature was cold and the gas cap on the rear deck froze shut. "We had to dig into our luggage and take out Kathy's hair dryer," Dennis remembered. "We asked the guy in the gas station where we could plug it in and we used it to melt the ice."

The T-Top coupe has the optional L46 350-cid, 350-hp V-8 and a four-speed manual gearbox. It also has a removable rear window, a luggage rack and fiber optics to monitor head and tail lamps.

"It gobbles up highway like you can't believe," according to Dennis. The new-car sticker price was $5,500, but Dennis paid the used car price of $4,500.

Originally finished in a turquoise blue color, the car was car repainted a darker blue in 1973.

"That was the year a driver in Madison, Wis., didn't see us change lanes," Dennis recalls. "After we got hit, we had it refinished in lacquer in a color we liked, but it's still our Blue Hawaii car." Dennis has also had the engine rebuilt due to problems with a broken piston ring. Today, the car is used infrequently and well preserved. It looks and runs just like it did when Dennis took it out of normal service.

Dennis and Kathy Bickford are veteran vendors at the Iola Old Car Show. Each year, you'll find them set up in the giant flea market on the first row north of the show's landmark forest ranger tower, right along the fence line east of *Old Cars Weekly's* east parking lot. That's where they promote the restoration services they offer, including wood car rebuilding, wood veneering, trim and upholstery, as well as custom-made convertible top installations.

CHAPTER 30 / 1970s NOVA
Story by Tom Collins

SOMETHING FOR EVERYBODY
The long-running Nova was a versatile role player

The Nova of the 1970s was born from the Chevy II of the 1960s.

There are some interesting statistics when it comes to 1970s Chevrolets. It seems those 1970s Caprices and Impalas disappeared in a manner that was disproportionate to their sales figures. Perhaps, like my parents' 1973 green Impala sedan, the cars were simply traded in on newer models and were well used in their later years.

I'd moved away from home when they purchased their 1973 Impala. My memories of that era were focused on another Chevrolet product, the Nova, because I had one as my first car.

By the 1970s, the Chevy II, introduced for the 1962 model year, had gone through the 1960s in various economical and muscular roles, but still was usually overshadowed by the full-size Chevrolets, the flashy

Corvette, the popular Chevelle and the spirited Camaro.

Even with its official name changed to Nova for the 1969 model year — a name originally used for the top-model line of the Chevy II — the small Chevy played second fiddle to the Monte Carlo, Vega and then even the Chevette in Chevrolet advertising.

But the Chevy II and Nova had a loyal following, especially from the mid-1960s on, among those who realized that its light weight combined with Chevrolet's assortment of engines meant a potent little screamer.

The early Chevy II and later Novas always retained a reputation for versatility. They could be plain and economical or quite powerful, and could be loaded with options. The 1968 re-design brought a stylish coupe body that aged well over five model years.

My neighbor, a Chevrolet-Olds dealer, knew that I was ready to buy my first car, a Placer Gold coupe. My first car looked just like the one featured on the 1972 Nova brochure, except it had full wheelcovers in place of the Rallye wheels.

My Nova came with the base 307-cid V-8, Powerglide automatic transmission, AM radio with a rear seat speaker, custom trim and tinted glass. I've heard all about Novas with the bigger engines, but my car was pretty fast. The light weight and V-8 meant plenty of pick-up when it was needed.

The Nova took me to my first job, teaching in Green Bay, Wis., then on a honeymoon after marriage in 1973 and to graduate school at the University of Missouri in 1974. My wife and I had our Nova until we purchased another car in 1978. Then my father-in-law used it for his short commute to work in Green Bay.

Novas filled many roles for others in the 1970s. When the muscle car craze was dampened by a combination of stiffer insurance costs, increased federal air pollution regulations and the oil crisis of 1973 and its consequent higher prices, the Nova once again proved to be an adaptable performer in the Chevrolet lineup that was easily repositioned as an economical choice.

In 1973, the hatchback version debuted, a clever design that simply married the long, slanted rear window with the trunk lid. The result was ample space in back with the rear seats folded.

When the 1973 Chevrolets debuted, I recall checking out a Nova hatchback and admiring how much room was gained by the conversion and the ability to fold the rear seat. The Chevrolet ad writers positioned the reconfiguration as the "Nova Motel."

And it wasn't long before Chevrolet saw the potential of the opened hatch by offering a covering they called the Hatchback Hutch. It turned the Hatchback into a camper for two.

In 1975, RPO Z11 turned the Nova into the Nova LN, a version that offered a plush interior and different trim, including upscale wheelcovers. For the next few years,

Chevrolet continued that tangent with the Concours. It was as if the Nova had a fashion makeover.

In 1976, Chevrolet introduced three special editions commemorating the American bicentennial. An Impala Sport Coupe and a Vega hatchback were offered, along with what was arguably the better-looking version of the three, the Nova Spirit of America. Each car was white with unique logos, red-and-blue trim and white seats with red-and-blue accents inside.

In 1975, Novas began emerging as valued police patrol vehicles, especially when results of the Los Angeles County Sheriff's Department testing were publicized. Traditional police cruisers had been larger Fords, Plymouths and Dodges in that era. The typical police versions were set up to be all-out pursuit vehicles.

But the L.A. County tests folded in elements of economy and overall reliability in their testing, in addition to the pursuit categories, and the newcomer Nova entry beat all the competition. Suddenly, police departments large and small saw the Nova in a new light, and Chevrolet was able to find one more role for their versatile cars.

Interestingly, the 1962 Chevy IIs had been offered with a rare police car option along with the Corvair. Both were available in six-cylinder varieties only. Wonder how many of either of those cars were purchased or survive today?

By the 1979 model year, new technology and increased fuel efficiency mandates meant all Chevrolets had been downsized or otherwise offered new designs. Chevrolet became a part of those trends and joined the General Motors push to introduce the X platform, their initial foray into versatile, economical front-wheel-drive cars.

Nova, Chevrolet's answer to the economy car demands of the late 1950s and early 1960s, retired from the automotive stage officially after 1979, yet the car has never really gone away for those of us who owned a new version or who bought one to restore or customize.

Many 1970s Chevrolet memories are wrapped around the versatile Nova. They found a place in our driveways and were the stars — and often continue to play starring roles — in our garages, shops and car-loving hearts.

1971 RALLY NOVA

By Phil Hall

FLASH OVER DASH

Graphics and color begain trumping horsepwer in muscle car era's final days

Arriving mid-year in 1971 was the Chevrolet Heavy Chevy option for the Chevelle Malibu two-door hardtop. It featured a hood and a few other cues from the SS, watered-down power, and, of course, graphics. (Phil Hall collection)

With the muscle car era in decline, domestic manufacturers weren't about to fold their tents in regards to offerings that might attract the horde of young buyers that once supported the market for tire-burning, big-engine screamers of the 1960s.

Thus, in a forest full of high insurance rates, emission regulations and federal safety demands, the muscle car torch was gradually passed to a new breed of muscle cars. This younger generation relied more on graphics than horsepower to draw the attention of the populace as the 1970s settled in. It is not that there weren't lower-horsepower youth cars before, like the 1970 Oldsmobile Cutlass Rallye 350, Pontiac Tempest GT-37, and Plymouth Valiant Duster 340, it's just that they became increasingly necessary to maintain sales volume.

At first, the new graphics cars could be

Making the full transition from performance to basic compact was the mid-year 1971 Chevrolet Rally Nova option. Striping, wheels, and a grille said "muscle," while power under the hood went from some promise in 1971 to mundane for 1972. (Phil Hall collection)

optioned with decent-performing engines, but as the dreadful decade wore on, more relied on gingerbread to make up for what was no longer available under the hood (the last Plymouth Volare Road Runners are a case in point).

For Chevrolet, it had a good thing going with its Super Sport versions of several models. However, Chevrolet never really answered the 1968 Plymouth Belvedere Road Runner with a budget muscle car, like Dodge, Ford, Mercury, Oldsmobile and Pontiac did.

Not all Super Sports from Chevrolet had the biggest engines, like the Chevelle SS-454, but all were classed as performance cars in the 1960s. For 1971, as muscle car sales dwindled and emission standards took hold, General Motors lowered compression ratios so that all cars could burn regular gasoline. Ford and Chrysler made partial cutbacks as the model year progressed.

To make matters worse, advertised horsepower ratings, once a game of great sport in exaggerating and underrating, went from gross to net. For example, the SS-454 was rated at 365 gross horses for 1971. The net equivalent was now 285 horses. In the 1960s, 7-liter engines were commonly advertised at 425 gross horsepower… and higher. The bragging factor was severely compromised by 1971.

A double dose of the new reality came from Chevy at the 1971 Chicago Auto Show. Two new options were introduced: the Heavy Chevy Chevelle and the Rally Nova. Both were watered-down versions of muscle cars, and both carried stripes and other effects and could be mechanically enhanced from a little to a little more.

They were added to the Chevrolet production lines in spring of that year and remained in place during the following 1972 model run, which featured little changed designs for both models.

Outside, the Heavy Chevy more or less

looked the part with its raised Super Sport hood, held down in front with the obligatory hood pins. A stripe down the side, blacked-out grille, plain steel rally wheels and decal identification completed the option, which came only on the Malibu two-door hardtop. Engines were nothing special and started with the 307-cid V-8, went through the 350-cid engine, and stopped with the 400-cid small-block. Cowl induction was an option.

The Nova side of the duo was marked by the Rally Nova option for the two-door sedan. Nova had been emasculated for 1971, losing its big-block V-8 as a regular production option. The SS option only went up to the 350-cid V-8.

Side and rear striping, a blacked-out grille, steel rally wheels and a 165-net-hp 350-cid V-8 were part of the Rally Nova package. In reality, a Rally Nova could be more potent than a Heavy Chevy, being lighter and having a larger engine standard.

For 1972, the Rally Nova option was reduced to any engine, meaning it was purely a graphics car. Neither the Heavy Chevy or Rally Nova options returned for 1973. The Chevelle was all-new, and the Nova underwent a mild facelift. However, the graphics cars would be with us for (too) many years to come.

Collectors today are hardly aware of the Heavy Chevy and Rally Nova. They do not command a significant premium over the base model prices, though cowl induction-equipped, 400-cid Heavy Chevys and 1971 Rally Nova 350s are rare and provide an alternative to the premium-priced SS versions.

1975 CHEVYS

By Mitch Frumkin

A MODEL YEAR
Chevrolet had good things cooking in 1975

Chevrolet's Corvette, America's only true production sports car at the time, added a new soft-face front bumper, but dropped the 454-cid V-8 for 1975. The base engine was a 350-cid V-8. Highlights of the Camaro were a wrap-around rear window, and on the Type LT (lower photo), more luxurious leather-trimmed interiors.

As Chevrolet Motor Division unveiled the 1975 models, the company indicated that the upcoming 12 months would mark one of the most significant years of product development in its history. Unveiled Sept. 27, 1974, in dealers' showrooms from coast-to-coast, the 1975 Chevrolet offered 46 models in eight different car lines.

In other words, "all kinds of cars for all

The 1975 Monte Carlo Landau coupe (top photo) featured a newly designed grid-pattern grille up front and new wrap-around taillamps in the rear. Adding to its prestige in the intermediate field for 1975, the Chevelle Malibu Classic (lower photo) gained ride and handling with suspension refinements and distinctive styling.

kinds of people."

These included memorable model nameplates no long in use — Caprice, Nova, Monza, and Camaro (coming back for 2009). Brands that have survived since 1975 are Corvette, Impala, Malibu and Monte Carlo.

Chevy had two pacesetters in its 1975 fleet: the all-new Monza 2+2 subcompact, and the completely re-designed Nova.

Reflecting European styling, the Monza 2+2 was a sporty hatchback. It featured trend-setting twin rectangular headlamps, functional B-pillar louvers and wrap-around rear lamps.

The 1975 Monza 2+2 came with an inte-

The full-size Caprice Classic four-door hardtop (top photo) offered a new level of luxury for 1975; its redesigned roof and distinctive grille set it apart from the Impala four-door sedan (lower photo).

gral frame and body design. Its 179.3-inch length was nearly four inches longer than the Vega. Both Monza and Vega were H-body subcompacts.

During mid-year, Chevy released a second Monza model. It was the Towne Coupe notchback, which had single round headlamps and a different instrument panel than the 2+2.

Nova, Chevrolet's compact, underwent one of the most extensive model-year changes since it was introduced as the Chevy II in 1962.

A big improvement on the Nova for 1975 was the replacement of the old front suspension system with the upgraded components used on the Camaro.

Nova was offered in both two-and four-door configurations. Its new look included greater glass area and flatter roofs.

For 1975, a top-of-the-line Luxury Nova (LN) Coupe and Sedan model was available, as well as a sportier SS coupe.

Differentiating the full-size Caprice

138

models from Impalas/Bel Airs, Chevy stylists created separate rooflines, each with larger side-viewing areas, as well as individual grille designs. The Caprice also had fender skirts and bright wheel moldings. There were a total of 15 models in the Caprice Classic and Estate, Impala and Bel Air line.

Chevelle, the intermediate-size Chevy, offered 11 models for 1975, including Malibu and top-of-line Malibu Classic series. Arriving in January 1975 was the (Malibu) Laguna Type S-3 sport/luxury coupe. Unique front styling cues distinguished the various Malibu models.

All Chevelles came with improved down-the-road tracking for better ride and handling gains

One of America's most popular personal cars, the Monte Carlo, wore new front styling with a re-styled grille and wrap-around rear tail lamps. Greater luxury interiors on the Monte Carlo offered a choice of standard bench, swivel buckets or optional 50-50 reclining passenger seats.

Monte Carlo came as V-8-powered coupe or Landau coupe versions.

Subcompact Vega retained its distinctive style for 1975, but boasted a list of 268 under-the-skin new parts and accessories. They ranged from engine and suspension equipment to new power brake and tilt steering wheel options.

Vega was available as a standard notchback and hatchback coupe, wagon, LX notchback and Estate wagon, GT Estate wagon, GT sport hatchback and wagon, and the double overhead-cam, fuel-injection four-cylinder Cosworth model.

Other station wagons available for 1975 included the full-size Chevrolet and the intermediate Chevelle of the two- and three-seat variety.

Camaro, Chevy's pony car, was sold as a regular sport coupe, luxury Type LT and performance Rally Sport. Gone was the Z-28 model. All Camaros featured a new wrap-around rear window.

Saving the best for last, the 1975 Corvette two-door coupe and convertible had upgrade chassis components, and was still America's only true sports car. Visually, the 'Vette wore a soft-face front bumper using honeycomb cell core with self-restoring feature, and the rear bumper employed hydraulic "enersorbers," an aluminum impact bar and urethane body color cover.

For 1975, Chevy issued a new small-block 262-cid V-8, which combined performance with fuel economy for use in the Monza 2+2. That engine was also teamed with the Nova as the base V-8.

The stock engine for Chevelle and standard Camaro models, and most Nova applications, was an improved 250-cid six-cylinder powerplant. It featured an integral cast inlet manifold and cylinder head design.

Both Camaro and Chevelle offered two versions of the 350-cid V-8 engines. An optional 235-horsepower, 454-cid V-8 was

For 1975, the subcompact Chevy Vega two-door station wagon (top photo) came powered by an aluminum-block, four-cylinder 140-cid engine with one-barrel carburetor, except for California where the otherwise optional two-barrel version was used. Brand new for 1975 was the all-new Monza 2+2 subcompact (lower photo) with twin rectangular headlamps and wrap-around rear lamps. It was four inches longer than the Vega.

available on the Chevelle, Monte Carlo and full-size Chevrolet.

The 454-big-block V-8 was dropped from the 1975 Corvette options, leaving the 165- or 205-horsepower 350 V-8's as the only engine choices. A 400-cid V-8 was the standard powerplant for the full-size Chevrolet wagons, while the 350-cid V-8 came equipped on the Chevelle wagons.

The heart of the extensive new vehicle systems design program for 1975 was a combination of mechanical advances designated as the "Chevrolet efficiency system." Beginning that model year, GM cars were outfitted with the underfloor catalytic converter. When the catalytic converter operated in conjunction with unleaded gasoline and factory tuning, the cars saw better response with fuel economy while achieving a considerable reduction in hydrocarbon and carbon monoxide emissions, as required by stringent federal emission regulations.

General Motors stated that before full

production, it thoroughly tested the catalytic converter in more than 1,000 cars, including taxis and government fleets, covering more than 20 million miles.

To improve the efficiency of carburetor models, Chevy devised a system that provided for the intake of cooler, denser air from the outside of the engine compartment and duct it to the carburetor for better performance. This outside air carburetion was on all vehicles except some six-cylinder Novas and the Monza 2+2 V-8 models.

Another new set-up for Chevrolet engines was called "Early Fuel Evaporation," which reduced stall and chugging when first starting out.

Standard for 1975 were longer-lasting, steel-belted radial-ply tires to improve traction on moisture and snow and reduce rolling resistance for improved gasoline mileage. These tires were on all Chevys, except Vega models, where they were optional.

Other components that could be ordered for greater fuel economy were special highway axle ratios that improved fuel consumption through a lower engine speed, and optional "Econominder" gauge package that included a manifold vacuum gauge to aid in driving for good fuel economy. One of Chevrolet's slogans was, "It runs leaner. It runs cleaner. It saves you money every mile."

An important benefit from the cleaner-burning unleaded fuel and Chevy's new ignition system in the 1975 models was extended service intervals. As an example, spark plug replacement interludes were increased from the former 6,000 miles to 22,500 miles.

F. James McDonald, General Motors vice president and Chevrolet general manager, said, "The new systems represent a giant step forward toward reaching our long-range goal of a 50,000-mile, no routine maintenance vehicle.

"What is more meaningful to the customer is that the system's components work together for significant improvements in fuel economy under normal driving conditions.

"We also estimate that it helps make possible savings in operations of about $100 a year and as much as $1,000 for the life of the car."

Chevy's model range has changed dramatically since 1975, and GM's number one division is working harder than ever against furious competition to convince 21st-century people to "see the U.S.A. in a Chevrolet."

Why Danchuk?

7 UNDISPUTABLE REASONS TO BUY DANCHUK PARTS:

1. We manufacture more parts than anyone in the industry, with the largest in-house manufacturing staff and facility.

2. We manufacture hundreds of original reproductions, and carry hundreds more aftermarket parts, but rest assured that the parts we manufacture are made right here in the good ol' USA, Santa Ana, California to be exact.

3. Our parts are the best of the best, the highest quality available, at the most competitive prices, so you get the most for your money.

4. We have the largest inventory, with most orders filled and shipped within 24 hours.

5. Our phones are answered by an actual person, with knowledgeable technical support just moments away.

6. Family owned and operated for 30 Years.

7. We ship from two locations, California and Indiana which means it costs you less to get your orders faster!!

Call today for a catalog! $5 Refundable with first purchase.

(800) 260-0414

3201 S. STANDARD AVE.,
SANTA ANA, CA 92705
Tech: (714) 751-1957
Fax: (714) 850-1957
www.danchuk.com

PARTS & ACCESSORIES AVAILABLE FOR

67-81 CAMARO

67-81 FIREBIRD

64-87 CHEVELLE, MALIBU & EL CAMINO

COMING SOON
64-72 GTO, TEMPEST & LE MANS

Restoring American History

FREE COLOR CATALOG

67-81 CAMARO
67-81 FIREBIRD
64-87 CHEVELLE, MALIBU & EL CAMINO

COMING SOON
64-72 GTO, TEMPEST & LE MANS

CALL 24 HOURS
352-387-0021

National Parts Depot is proud to have been named "2009 Business of the Year" by the Automotive Restoration Market Organization. To be honored in this way only strengthens our resolve to lead the restoration parts industry in overall quality, customer service, speed, value and ethics. You can place faith in our performance.

National Parts Depot is proud to be a major sponsor of The Iacocca Foundation and The Lee Iacocca Award, "Given for Dedication to excellence in perpetuating an American Automotive Tradition."

www.iacoccafoundation.org

FOUR FULLY-STOCKED WAREHOUSES/STORES
OVER **570,000** square foot

MICHIGAN, Canton
800-521-6104
734-397-4569 - 2435 S. Haggerty Rd.

N. CAROLINA, Charlotte
800-368-6451
704-331-0900 - 7000 MacFarlane Blvd.

FLORIDA, Ocala
800-874-7595
352-861-8700 - 900 SW 38th Ave.

CALIFORNIA, Ventura
800-235-3445
805-654-0468 - 1376 Walter St. #1

NPD
NATIONAL PARTS DEPOT

www.NATIONALPARTSDEPOT.com

See What it Takes to be a SURVIVOR Car

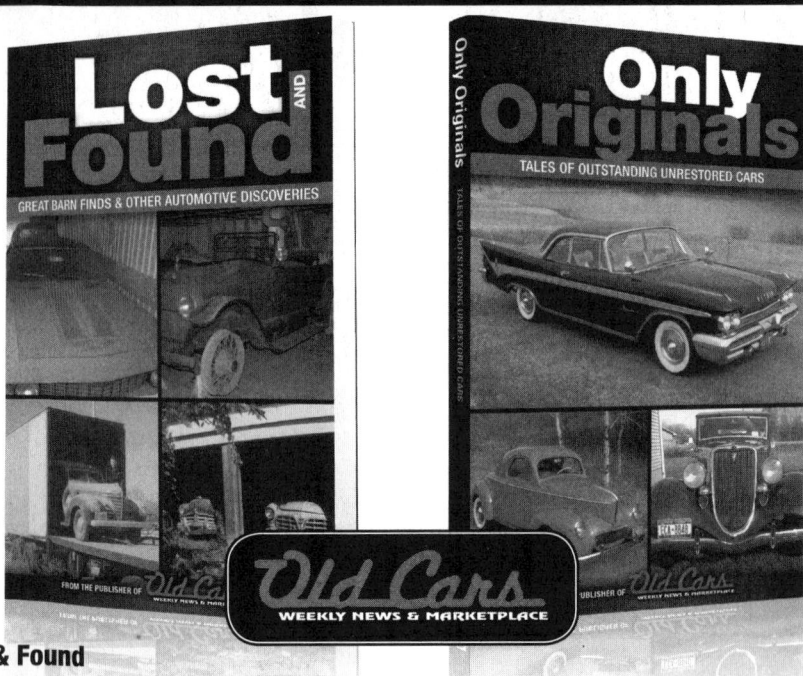

Lost & Found
Great Barn Finds & Other Automotive Discoveries
By the editors of Old Cars Weekly

Lost & Found is filled with feel good true stories of old cars that been discovered after lengthy slumbers in everything from barns to semi trailers. This collection is not just the "dream car" stories of Duesenbergs and Hemi muscle cars, but the common man's Chevy's, Fords and Chryslers that so many hobbyists own and love. You never know where a great old car might be hiding!
Softcover • 6x9 • 144 pages
Item #Z8817 • $12.99

Only Originals
Outstanding Unrestored Cars
By the editors of Old Cars Weekly

In Only Originals, collector car fans can examine a fascinating cross selection of survivor cars and learn how they have managed to defy the odds. From Duesenbergs to Corvettes, this book salutes the unrestored, "time capsule" cars that remind us of yesterday.
Softcover • 6x9 • 144 pages
Item #Z8818 • $12.99

Order online at **www.ShopOldCarsWeekly.com**
Call **800-258-0929**

kp krause publications
A division of F+W Media, Inc.
700 East State Street • Iola, WI 54990-0001